Seven Perspectives on ❧ the Woodcut ❧

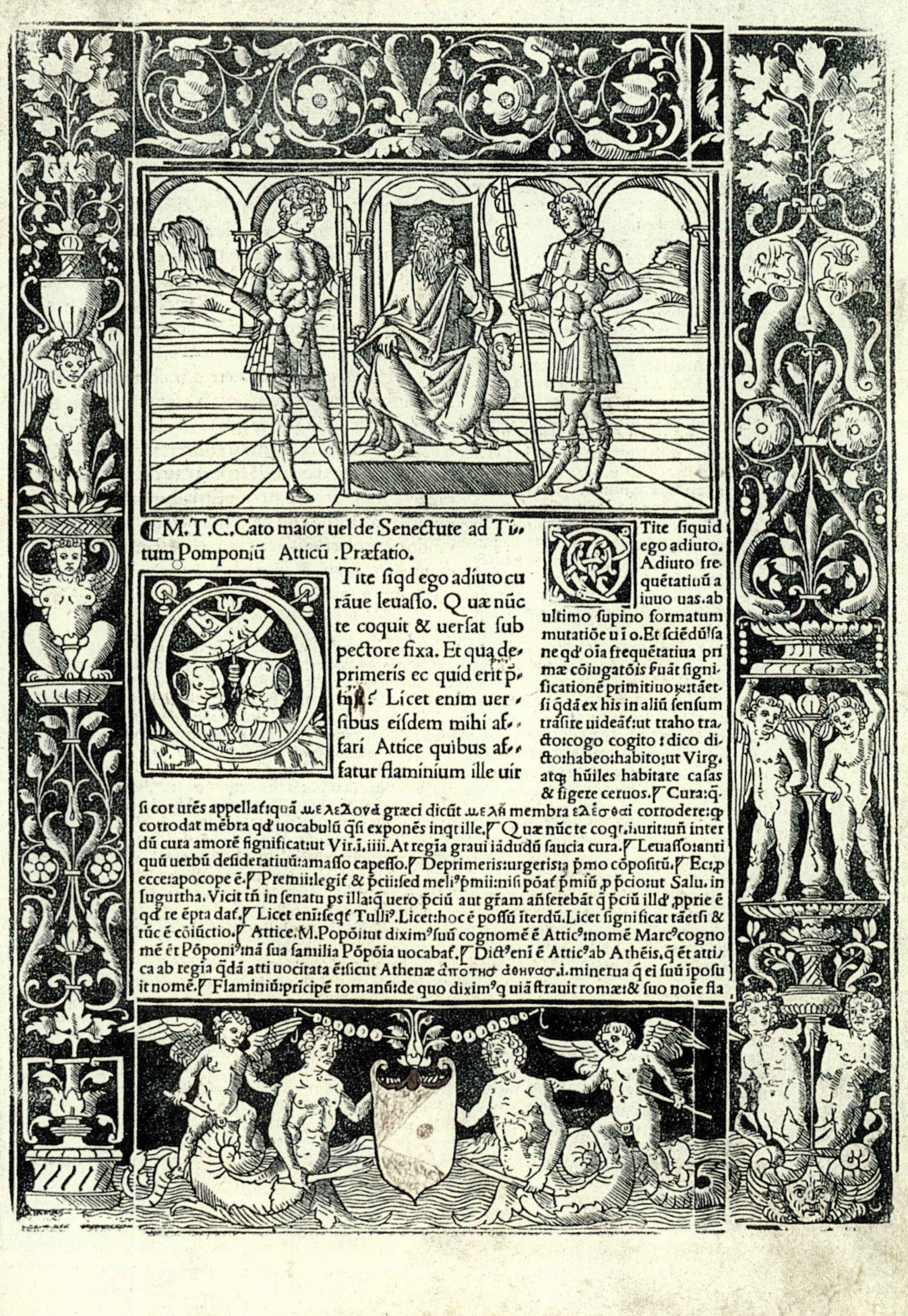

¶ M.T.C. Cato maior uel de Senectute ad Titum Pomponiũ Atticũ. Præfatio.

O Tite ſiqd ego adiuto curãue leuaſſo. Quæ nũc te coquit & uerſat ſub pectore fixa. Et quã depſſeris ec quid erit pmii? Licet enim uerſibus eiſdem mihi affari Attice quibus affatur flaminium ille uir

O Tite ſiquid ego adiuto. Adiuto frequẽtatiuũ a iuuo uas. ab ultimo ſupino formatum mutatiõe u i o. Et ſciẽdũ ſane qđ oĩa frequẽtatiua primæ cõiugatõis ſuãt ſignificationẽ primitiuo ꝝ: tãetſi q̃dã ex his in aliũ ſenſum trãſire uideãt: ut traho tracto: cogo cogito: dico dicto: habeo: habito: ut Virg. atq; hũiles habitare caſas & figere ceruos. ¶ Cura: q̃. ſi cor urẽs appellat: quã μελεδονα græci dicũt μελη membra εδεσθαι corrodere: q̃ corrodat mẽbra qđ uocabulũ q̃ſi exponẽs inqt ille. ¶ Quæ nũc te coqt. i. urit: uñ interdũ cura amorẽ ſignificat: ut Vir. i. iiii. At regia graui iãdudũ ſaucia cura. ¶ Leuaſſo: anti quũ uerbũ deſideratiuũ: amaſſo capeſſo. ¶ Deprimeris: urgeris: a p̄mo cõpoſitũ. ¶ Ec: p ecce: apocope ẽ. ¶ Premii: legit & p̄cii: ſed meli⁹ p̄mii: niſi põat p̄miũ p p̄cio: ut Salu. in Iugurtha. Vicit tñ in ſenatu ps illa: q̃ uero p̄ciũ aut grãm añferebãt q̃ p̄ciũ illđ pprie ẽ qđ re ẽpta dat. ¶ Licet eni: ſeqt Tulli⁹. Licet: hoc ẽ poſſũ iterdũ. Licet ſignificat tãetſi & tũc ẽ cõiũctio. ¶ Attice. M. Popõi: ut dixim⁹ ſuũ cognomẽ ẽ Attic⁹: nomẽ Marc⁹ cognomẽ ẽt Põponi⁹: nã ſua familia Põpõia uocabat. ¶ Dict⁹ eni ẽ Attic⁹ ab Athẽis. q̃ ẽt attica ab regia q̃dã atti uocitata ẽ: ſicut Athenæ ἀπο της ἀθηνας. i. minerua q̃ ei ſuũ ĩpoſuit nomẽ. ¶ Flaminiũ: pricipẽ romanũ: de quo dixim⁹ q uiã ſtrauit romæ: & ſuo noie fla

Seven Perspectives on the Woodcut

Presentations from
A Heavenly Craft
Symposium and Exhibition

Edited by Daniel De Simone

Curator, Lessing J. Rosenwald Collection

Library of Congress

Library of Congress, 2008

LIBRARY OF CONGRESS
Director of Publishing: W. Ralph Eubanks
Editor: Wilson McBee

Index: Kate Mertes, Mertes Editorial Services, Alexandria, Virginia
Book design: Patricia Inglis, Inglis Design, Galesville, Maryland

LIBRARY OF CONGRESS CATALOGING-IN-PUBLICATION DATA

Seven perspectives on the woodcut / edited by Daniel De Simone.
p. cm.
Presentations from "A Heavenly Craft" symposium and exhibition
April 21, 2005, at the Library of Congress, Washington, D.C.
Includes bibliographical references and index.
ISBN 978-0-8444-1183-5 (alk. paper)
1. Wood-engraving—15th century—Congresses. 2. Wood-engraving—
16th century—Congresses. I. De Simone, Daniel.
NE1050.S48 2008
761'.209024
2007043992

See Library of Congress online collections at
<www.loc.gov>

Printed in China

Contents

Introduction

On april 21, 2005, the Rare Book and Special Collections Division of the Library of Congress was privileged to host a symposium celebrating the exhibition *A Heavenly Craft: The Woodcut in Early Printed Books.* Lessing J. Rosenwald, retired chairman of Sears, Roebuck & Company, purchased the books in the exhibition at the sale of the library of the British collector C. W. Dyson Perrins (1864–1958), heir to the Lea & Perrins fortune. The books were donated to the Library of Congress as part of Mr. Rosenwald's larger gift of illustrated books, a collection considered to be one of the most important private libraries formed in the twentieth century. The exhibition was organized to celebrate Mr. Rosenwald's gift and to explore the history of the woodcut during the first decades of printing. It was hoped that, by examining the subject from both a bibliographical and an art historical perspective, new insights might emerge about the development of the art form.

The exhibition documented the artistic development of the woodcut as it evolved in Augsburg, Ulm, Nuremberg, and the Low Countries, and then as it spread south of the Alps to Venice, Florence, Rome, Paris, and the Iberian peninsula. The exhibition opened at the Grolier Club in New York in December of 2004, traveled back to the Library of Congress for an opening the following April, and then concluded its tour in Dallas, where it was on display at the Bridwell Library, Southern Methodist University, from September to December of 2005. An illustrated catalogue with detailed descriptions of each of the items on display accompanied the exhibition. The catalogue also included scholarly essays by Paul Needham, Lilian Armstrong, and Daniela Laube. Paul Needham is the Scheide Librarian at Princeton University and a noted Gutenberg scholar who has published extensively on early printed books. Lilian Armstrong, the Mildred Lane Kemper Professor of Art at Wellesley College, is a well-known scholar of Venetian miniature painters and author of books and articles on the Putti Master, the Pico Master, and Benedetto Bordon. Daniela Laube is a third-generation print seller from Zurich, and now New York, who specializes in old master prints, modern prints, drawings, rare books, and Helvetica. Needham's essay examined Mr. Rosenwald's participation in the Dyson Perrins auction sale and discussed in some detail the nature of his important gift to the Library of Congress. Drawing on her research on Venetian illuminated manuscripts, Armstrong focused her essay on the Venetian and Florentine woodcuts and the sources of their design from the manuscript tradition. Laube's essay discussed the stylistic development of the German woodcut from 1461 to 1500 as well as the evolution of woodcut style throughout Europe.

The symposium of April 2005 was organized with the support of the Gladys Krieble Delmas Foundation, which endorsed our desire to explore more fully some of the themes described in the exhibition catalogue. It was our intention to create a public dialogue between historians of the book and art historians about the woodcut's transition in style from the late medieval to the Renaissance period. In doing so we wanted to highlight the research of a distinguished group of scholars on the subjects of manuscript illumination, early printed books, and the single leaf woodcut.

The morning session of the symposium began with a presentation by Richard S. Field, Curator Emeritus of Prints, Drawings, and Photographs at Yale University Art Gallery and former Curator of the Lessing J. Rosenwald Collection. His paper is entitled "The Woodcuts and Woodblocks of Albrecht Dürer: Inspiration, Standardization, and Reformation of an Art." Lilian Armstrong followed with a paper entitled "Woodcuts in Classical Texts Printed in Venice, 1490–1520, and the Role of Benedetto Bordon as a Designer." Peter Stallybrass delivered the final presentation of the morning session. He is the Walter H. and Leonore C. Annenberg Professor in the Humanities at University of Pennsylvania, and the title of his discussion was "Image against Text: On Not Reading *Genesis*."

In the afternoon, panelists continued the discussion of the early woodcut with discussions of specific examples of its evolving style. Helena Szépe, Associate Professor of Art at the University of South Florida, presented the first talk, entitled "Benedetto Bordon and Venetian *Ducali*." She was followed by Eric Marshall White, Curator of Special Collections at the Bridwell Library, Southern Methodist University, whose address was titled "The Woodcuts in Breydenbach's *Peregrinatio* and the Limits of Fifteenth-Century Empiricism." Jeffrey F. Hamburger, Professor of Art and Architectural History at the Sackler Museum, Harvard University, was next with a talk entitled "From Print to Manuscript: The Interaction of Incunabula and Illumination after the Invention of Printing." I concluded the day's discussion with my presentation entitled "Stylistic Influences on Ferrarese Woodcut Design at the End of the Fifteenth Century." We were fortunate to have a large attendance of rare book librarians, curators, collectors, and dealers who participated in the question and answer sessions with an enthusiasm rarely witnessed at such events.

This Symposium Report includes the full text of the presentations made by our morning panelists and synopses of the presentations made in the afternoon sessions. Mindful of the visual nature of the content of the symposium, we have included nearly fifty illustrations dispersed throughout the text. These images will remind those who attended the symposium of the power of the panelists' presentations. For those who were unable to come to Washington, the images should create a visual timeline that documents the evolution of the woodcut and the development of the Renaissance style.

Die neunundtreyssigist figur

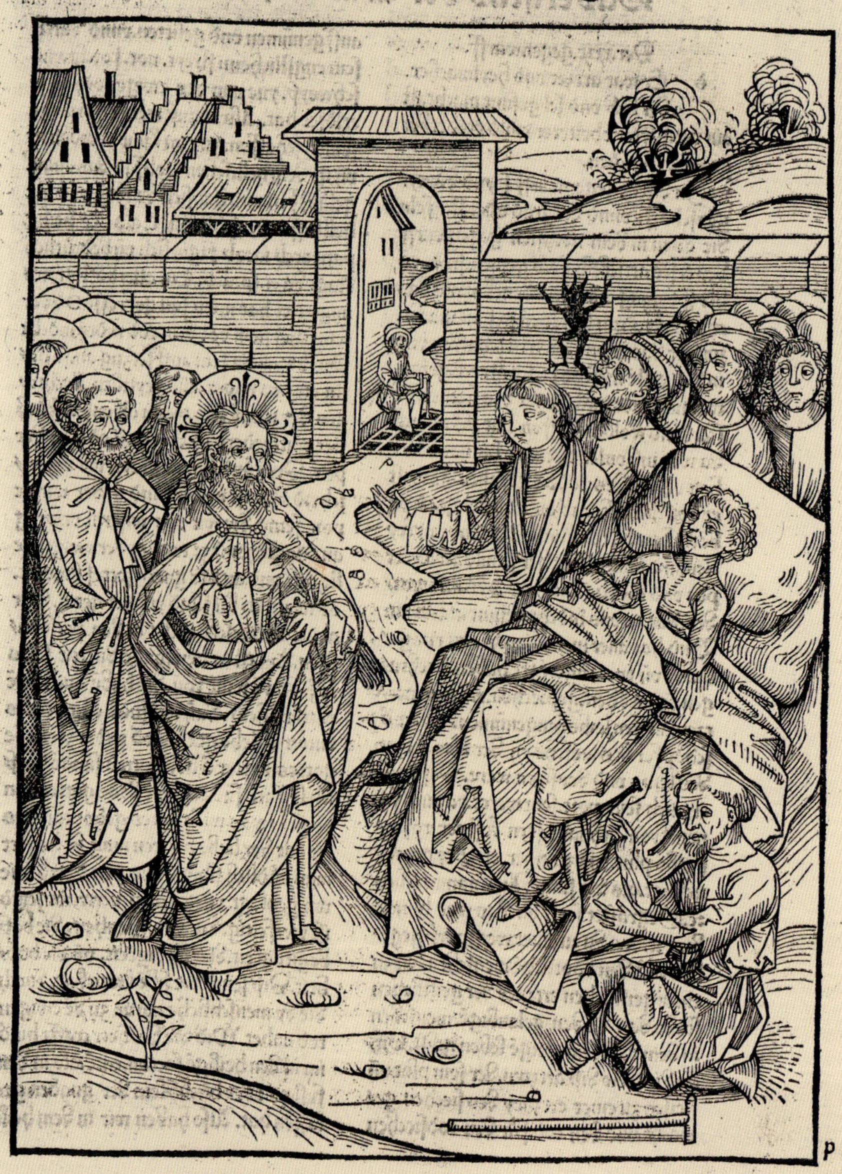

p ij

Richard S. Field

The Woodcuts and Woodblocks of Albrecht Dürer: Inspiration, Standardization, and Reformation of an Art

The following paragraphs form as much a report as an essay. Daniel De Simone asked me to devise a lecture that would serve as an introduction to this woodcut symposium and focus primarily on the achievements of Albrecht Dürer. We decided that the talk would consist of three parts. The first delineates the development of Dürer's incomparable woodcuts, quickly reviewing the variety of his approaches but also noting the emergence of a standardized workshop technique that would serve as the touchstone for woodcut production during the next 350 years. The second offers a few comparisons with woodcuts by Dürer's contemporaries, not simply to manifest the impact of the master's formulations but also to suggest the highly creative languages of a few of his gifted contemporaries. The final section offers a recapitulation of the first, but this time through an examination of the woodblocks that were responsible for the printed images. This represents the beginnings of an investigation that my colleague Shelley Fletcher and I intend to develop into a detailed study of surviving fifteenth-century woodblocks. My remarks touch upon a subject that was hotly debated from the late eighteenth through the middle of the twentieth century: did Dürer cut his own blocks?

I.

Many of the characteristic qualities of the best German woodcuts of 1460–80—the generation preceding Albrecht Dürer's—are represented by a Flagellation from the Berlin Kupferstichkabinett.[1] The overwhelming impact of this work is one of direct communication, a bare-bones relationship between the viewer and a familiar subject. Little is here that does not serve the ghoulish perversity of Christ's tormentors. Despite the curving contours, the image is composed of lines that delineate angular and

Fig. 1. Michael Wolgemut. Christ Healing the Sick, woodcut from Stephen Fridolin. *Schatzbehalter.* Nuremberg: Anton Koberger, 1491 (Rosenwald Collection 154, Library of Congress, Washington).

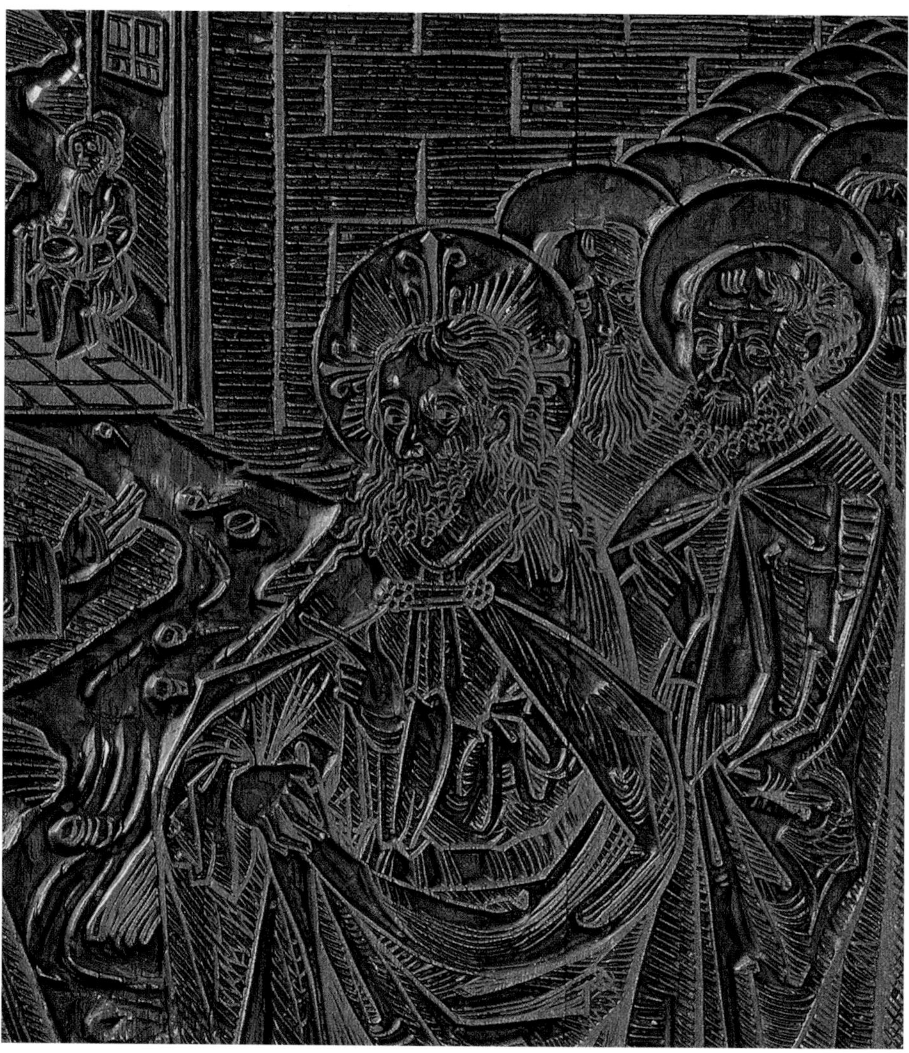

Fig. 2. Michael Wolgemut. Christ Healing the Sick, detail of the original woodblock for Stephen Fridolin. *Schatzbehalter*. Nuremberg: Anton Koberger, 1491 (Bildarchiv Preussischer Kulturbesitz / Art Resource, NY).

aggressive forms and features. The action is formulaic, with no passages describing subtleties of light, texture, setting, movement in space, or nuances of facial expression. Together with the emphatic framing and shallow space, the lines themselves are conditioned by the flat plane of the original surface of the block, reinforcing not just the anti-illusionistic and anti-realistic qualities of the woodcut, but its immediacy of meaning, its "foregrounding."[2]

During this period, however, the woodcut became much more descriptive, especially as it sought to depict more ambitious narratives with greater realism. This was accomplished through the addition of repeated short strokes that tend to blend with one another. Such systems of hatchings are more optical in nature than the simple, descriptive contours. A typical, if not particularly gracious, example is the woodcut Christ Healing the Sick, a page from Stephan Fridolin's *Schatzbehalter,* printed in 1491 by Dürer's godfather, Anton Koberger. Now the long contours—which Erwin Panofsky called "descriptive lines"—are accompanied by whole systems of shorter hatchings, Panofsky's "optical lines."[3] Both sets of lines are still marked by a pronounced angularity more appropriate to the portrayal of a crowded, agitated, and miraculous narrative than to pictorial grace. In this example, the technique of cutting yielded effects akin to the quick and unsubtle strokes of a pen, as in the beards, sleeves, and even faces. The hatching evokes some sensation of shading but hardly the "optical" pictorialisms of a sophisticated drawing. In works such as these, the application of color could still be crucial to distinguish larger passages, organize the entire image, and even suppress Late Gothic emotionalism, as a comparison with a hand-colored page from the *Schatzbehalter* demonstrates.

Although Dürer was involved in the designing of woodcuts during his years in Basel and Strasbourg (1491–93), he neither attempted radical changes to the medium nor worked closely with those who cut his blocks. On his return from his first trip to Italy in 1495, however, he was charged with the ambition to introduce the grace and rationality of Italian figure drawing into the traditional German woodcut. This demanded a hitherto unknown technical complexity and initiated a major reformation of the expectations of the medium. Dürer's Martyrdom of the Ten Thousand of ca. 1496, which depicts the forced death of Roman troops who had been converted to Christianity, is a great leap forward in harnessing the woodcut to pictorial ends. Not only are the basic contours curvilinear and spatial instead of angular and flat, but they are no longer bound to the planar qualities of the wood, having been set free to determine both the shapes and the edges of volumes. The contour is now a dynamic instrument, swelling and tapering as in the man with the scourge in the middle ground. A new organic and systematic handling of the hatching informs the multitude of nudes

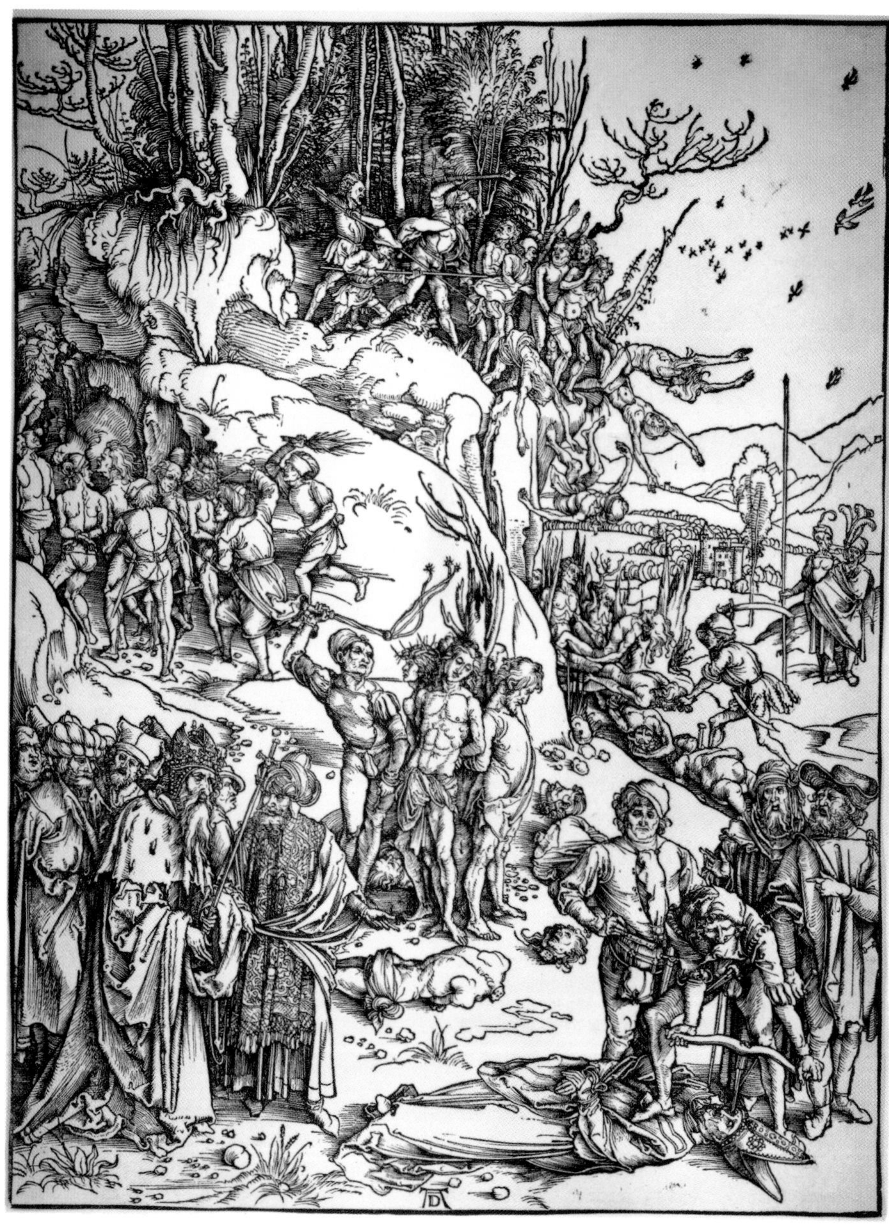

Fig. 3. Albrecht Dürer. Martyrdom of the Ten Thousand, woodcut, 1496–97 (Rosenwald Collection, National Gallery of Art. © Board of Trustees, National Gallery of Art, Washington). See Fig. 8 for original woodblock.

and articulates the hollowing out of draperies. Even more impressive is Dürer's construction of textures through the shaping of individual lines—the legs of the standing executioners at the lower right—and through the massing of a variety of optical lines, as in the highly decorative rendering of the Emperor's Turkish garments. Nonetheless, the composition remains crowded and busy, filled with action, gesture, and speech at the expense of overall organization. Since the artist's main attention is directed to the character of line, he has only begun to recognize that the white of the paper can serve as tone. One has the impression of an overly ambitious work; in fact, Dürer wrote that the theme itself would provide a perfect opportunity to represent the human form in all manner of positions.[4]

At about the same time that he was finishing the Martyrdom of the Ten Thousand, Dürer began to design his most innovative work, the *Apocalypse,* which, when completed in 1498, consisted of fifteen large images printed together with a continuous text. In its rendering of Saint John's visions, it surpassed all earlier printed versions in both imagination and execution. It achieved so perfect a balance between description and abstraction that it has persisted over the centuries as the most moving evocation of the text.[5] In the Apocalyptic Woman and the Seven-Headed Beast (Revelations 12:1–16) of 1496–97, Dürer began to recast the woodcut in terms of the nuances of the tonal and descriptive potential of copperplate engraving. Comparing the edges of the woman's wings with those in Martin Schongauer's engraving of the Angel of the Annunciation from the mid-1480s reveals how massed, fine lines provide a sense of soft and palpable rounding in space as well as convincing darkness, as in the deep crevices of the draperies. Dürer, himself already a master engraver, has fused the descriptive and optical functions of the woodcut vocabulary; line imparts volume, texture, tone, movement, and emotion to an extent that is clearly more technically advanced than in the Martyrdom of the Ten Thousand. Nevertheless, in its crowding, incessant graphic activity, and awkward white spaces of unprinted paper, the Apocalyptic Woman still reveals the insistent hold of the Late Gothic spirit. Over the next thirteen years the trajectory of Dürer's woodcuts would describe a stream of solutions aimed at dampening such excesses through a gradual simplification and rationalization of both style and technique.

Contemporaneous with the Apocalyptic Woman is the Entombment (or Deposition), an early work from Dürer's *Large Passion.* Contributing significantly to a clearer organization of the picture space is the enlargement of the main protagonists. Though the picture surface is still filled, it is less cluttered; a similar attempt to provide more breathing space also informs the larger interstices between hatchings and cross-hatchings. The white areas of the image are less haphazard and better integrated into the overall composition of lights and darks. Although stiffly rendered, faces and hands are imbued with greater character and expressiveness. Unexpectedly, they continue to bear traces of the exaggerated types that populated Michael Wolgemut's *Schatzbehalter* woodcuts, which might indicate that some of the same cutters were working with Dürer.[6] Despite the increased sense of space and atmosphere, the details reveal the artist's continuing fondness for a variety of graphic marks, an active "painterly" surface that simultaneously models, describes, and suggests texture. Similar impulses inform the gnarled tree trunks and twisted bodies—all very much pushed up against the picture plane, continuing to draw the viewer into an intimate and emotional relationship with the substance of the narrative.

A more pronounced sense of logical and peaceful organization pervades two slightly later works, Saint John Devouring the Book from the *Apocalypse* and the Lamentation from the *Large Passion*, both usually dated 1498. In the Saint John woodcut, the artificial separation of the heavenly and earthly realms (the fantastic and the natural) is reduced. Line itself is frequently clarified and generalized, as in the concave modeling of the rocks and draperies, the diagonals of the beams of light, the curly foliage, and the horizontal strata of clouds. Most significantly, the entire composition has been unified by the adoption of a single, low point of view, underscored by the progression of hand, tree trunk, and angel. In the Lamentation, the same clarity is now brought to bear on inner grief, that of the Virgin for her son, with which the viewer readily identifies. The impact of the woodcut is reinforced by the classically composed image: the strong central vertical, the pyramidal group in the foreground, and the diagonal axes. Late Gothic emotionalism has begun to give way to a more constrained and measured grief; even the expressions of the woman with the headband and the one who embraces her knee are tinged with classical suppression, as is the tender gesture of Mary Magdalene, who holds Christ's hand. The Virgin herself stands tall, quietly containing her sorrow.[7] More than that of the Saint John Devouring the Book, the technique of the Lamentation reiterates a sense of compression—the dampening of Late Gothic fussiness, particularity, friability, and the restricted, somber tone of the landscape. Perhaps it is here that one first senses the way passages of hatching and tone support the overall rhythms of the main figures, as the cross-hatched passages of the standing figure of the Virgin seem to gently sculpt her form. The Lamentation may be regarded as a rather undramatic image, but it introduces a sculptural and tonal sensibility that will gradually assume a pivotal role in Dürer's woodcuts.

While this presentation offers a view of the development of Dürer's woodcuts as an organic, linear progression, available space precludes any detailed discussion of the dating or sequencing of the thirty major blocks of 1495–1500, which included important experiments and byways. Similarly, only mention can be made of the nineteen woodcuts of the *Life of the Virgin* and the numerous, modest scale woodcuts that the artist probably included in the category he himself called "*schlecte Holzwerk*," perhaps best translated as "common woodcuts."[8]

The next comparison contrasts two woodcuts from the *Large Passion* that span the years from 1498 to 1510. The Bearing of the Cross of ca. 1498 and The Betrayal and Capture of Christ, dated 1510, offer a striking contrast of technique while still preserving Gothic preferences for crowded, foregrounded, rowdy, and even brutal representations of the Passion. In the earlier image, Christ emerges from the gates of Jerusalem into the light. The composition condenses many episodes: the bearing and falling under the cross, the assistance of Simon of Cyrene, and the compassion of Saint Veronica. The crowd surges to the right (as in all of the Passion scenes) but is dominated and restrained by the huge cross. Despite his burden, Christ's stability is secured by his left arm, which rests on a prominent stone (possibly a reference to Peter). It enables him to turn away from the crowd, under the protection of the cross, and to confront Veronica in a private moment torn from the agitation of the impending disaster of the Crucifixion. By contrast, the scene is also stamped with the striking indifference of the harlequin-like Italian soldier who faces away from the viewer, whom he may simultaneously personify. The soldier's great halberd acts as an exclamatory stop, providing the viewer with a moment to reexamine Christ's encounter with Veronica as well as the colorful and sordid types that have assembled to play out the conditions of the "human stain." So complex are Dürer's graphic ambitions, so filled with description of every kind is this woodcut, that only the very best impressions allow sufficient visual clarity for the image to be read. In poor impressions, the white interstices of the area bounded by Christ, Simon, and Veronica are too ill-defined to permit them to function as space, and the black lines too broken up to be read as form. The resulting cacophony of black and white disintegrates into an unintelligible muddle on the surface of the paper.

Late Gothic turbulence, emotionalism, and grotesqueness also inform the Betrayal of 1510, with its activated expressions of hatred and spite. But here Dürer's graphic technique embodies a new rationalism. Light bathes and unifies the entire scene, apparently from the single torch at the extreme right of the image. The whites of the paper are carefully orchestrated, and it is the illumination itself that articulates both the composition and its meaning. Hatchings are laid down in a more orderly fashion, their parallelism emphasized and their width carefully controlled, so that shaded areas project a luminous transparency in addition to their strictly tonal value. The composition is less dependent upon single contours—upon drawing with dark lines—and thrives on forms whose edges are defined by the shaded areas of hatching that lay "behind";

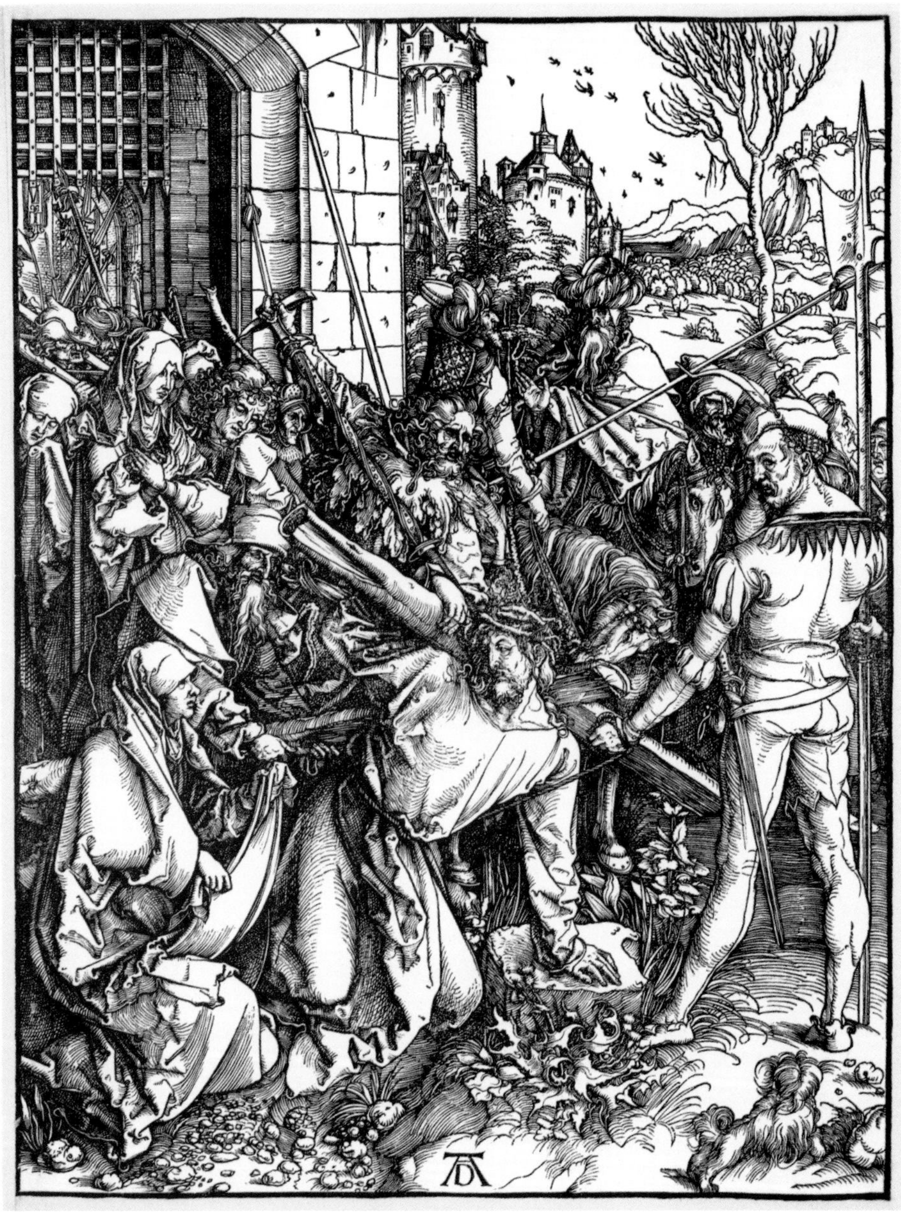

Fig. 4. Albrecht Dürer. Bearing of the Cross, woodcut, 1498 (Rosenwald Collection, National Gallery of Art. © Board of Trustees, National Gallery of Art, Washington).

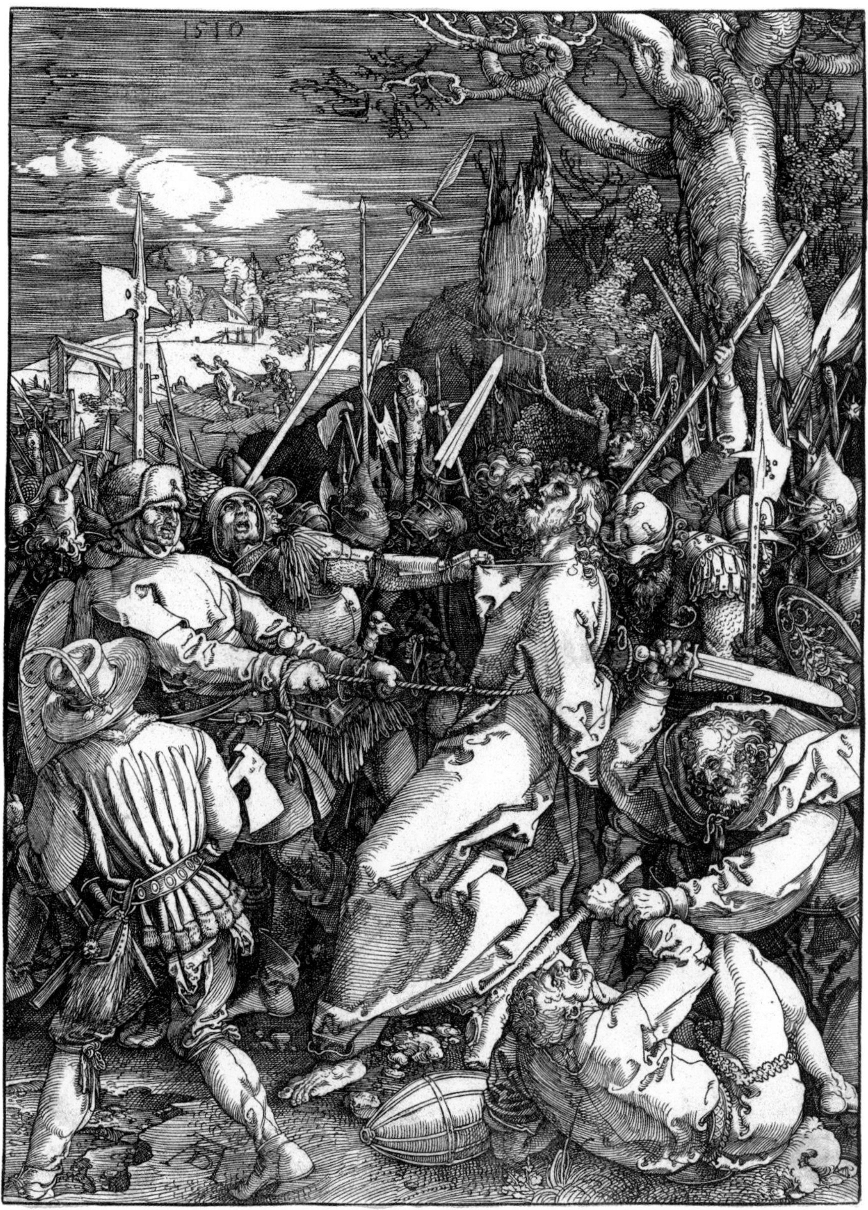

Fig. 5. Albrecht Dürer. Betrayal of Christ, woodcut, 1510 (Rosenwald Collection, National Gallery of Art. © Board of Trustees, National Gallery of Art, Washington).

increasingly, significant form migrates back and forth between isolated whites and regular passages of shadow. Most crucial, as Panofsky pointed out, are the areas of hatching and cross-hatching that evoke a neutral gray tonality, against which the lights and darks play out their dramatic roles. Despite its agitated composition, the broad pictorialism of the Betrayal sweeps aside the older dependency on individualized description that characterized the Bearing of the Cross.

The tri-tonal system (black, gray, and white) would not have been so effective had Dürer not also radically simplified his figure types, as in Christ's Descent into Limbo of 1511.[9] Note how the figures of Adam (with the cross) and Eve are rendered with evenly spaced, relatively unbroken lines and simultaneously "covered" with a fine overlay of completely nondescriptive, transparent hatching to embed them in the shadows of the background. Dürer and his cutters have devised a tonal system that supplanted the sculptural constructions of the late 1490s. Everything—space, volume, texture, description, movement—is subordinated to this new order, including the presence of dominant single figures, whose very physicality is ordered along classical principles of a dynamic balance of force and counterforce. In sum, the rationality of Dürer's accomplishments of 1510–11 achieved a fusion of Renaissance and Late Gothic ideals that provided models for his contemporaries and followers, from the most gifted to the most ordinary. Dürer's reformation of the woodcut remained the standard until the very end of the nineteenth century, when ideas about primitivism and the subconscious retrieved the medium's long-lost irrational roots.[10]

With these woodcuts of 1510–11, Dürer and his workshop seem to have reached a particularly pregnant formulation. Conceptually and technically, the three-tone system provided a straightforward method for woodcut production, one that might be exploited by the best artists and handily adopted by the less ambitious and less gifted, fueling popular, religious, and historical productions that stretched from the sixteenth through the nineteenth centuries. Typical of this synthesis is the Saint Christopher, dated 1511. Granted, its rather dry perfection—specifically in the uninflected passages of the landscape and the water—and the slightly mechanical look of the entire block seem to deprive the image of the vivacity and nervousness of the master's touch and have given pause to the attribution to Dürer himself.[11] This is not to say that the calligraphic, draftsmanly technique of the *Apocalypse* and the earlier blocks of the *Large Passion* ceased to provide inspiration—notably for the brilliant sixteenth-century woodcuts of Titian and his Venetian followers and for the seventeenth-century Netherlandish works by Christoffel Jegher and Jan Lievens.[12] In the main, however, it was the regularity, spatial clarity, volumetric capacity, and straightforward narrative potential of the 1511 synthesis that prevailed.

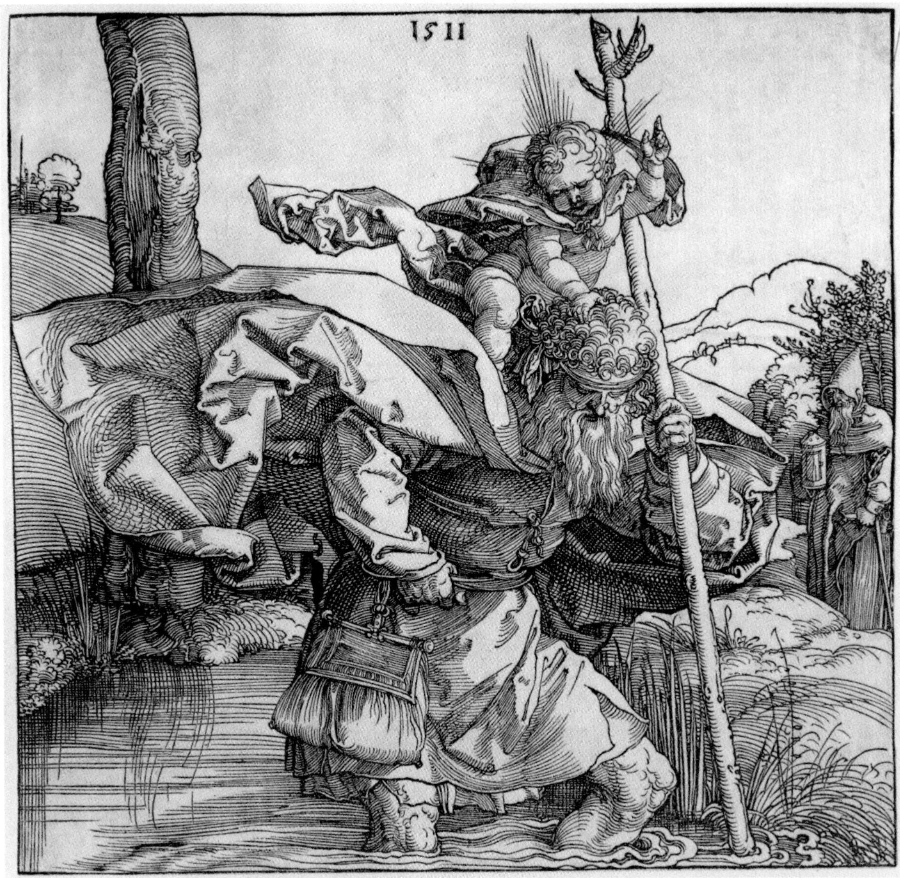

Fig. 6. Albrecht Dürer. Saint Christopher, woodcut, 1511 (Rosenwald Collection, National Gallery of Art. © Board of Trustees, National Gallery of Art, Washington).

II.

It would be easy to line up dozens of contemporaries—such as Leonhard Beck, Hans Sebald Beham, Urs Graf, Wolf Huber, Hans Süss von Kulmbach, Hans Leonhard Schäufelein, Hans Springinklee, Erhard Schön, and Wolf Traut—whose woodcuts were greatly indebted to Dürer's stylistic, iconographic, and technical innovations. More worthy of mention, however, are those who, inspired by Dürer, forged strikingly original woodcuts of their own. Probably the earliest of these was Lucas Cranach, whose Crucifixion of 1502 is nearly Baroque in its emotional exuberance. Clearly derived from Dürer's Crucifixion of 1497–98, it outdistances its forerunner in its emphatic sense of organic growth and movement. Dürer's symmetry is replaced by dynamic, even tortured spatial dislocations, typified by the figures of the two thieves. By comparison with these

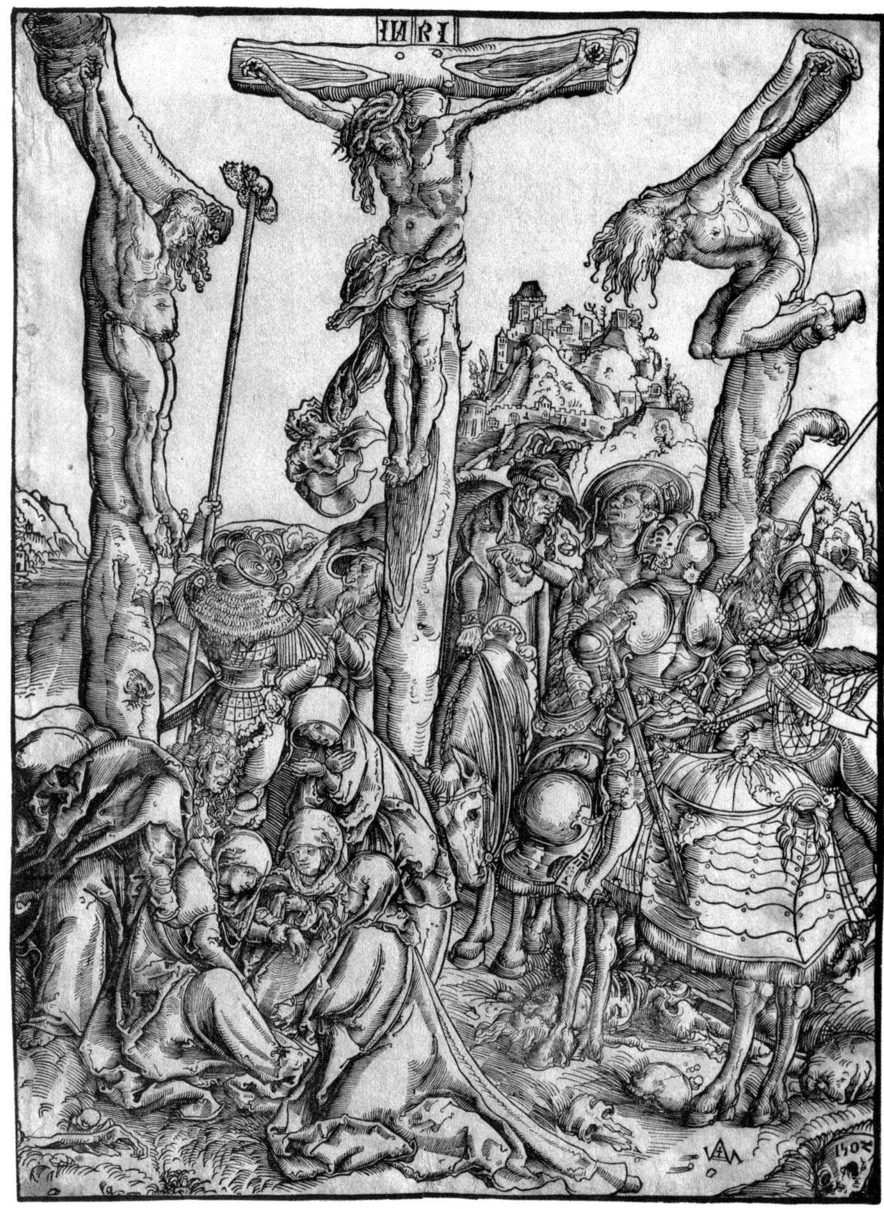

Fig. 7. Lucas Cranach the Elder. Calvary, woodcut, 1502 (The Metropolitcan Museum of Art, Harris Brisbane Dick Fund, 1927. 27.54.3. Image © The Metropolitan Museum of Art).

nervous and pulsating figures, Dürer's are flat and staid, their emotions signified rather than dramatized. The knobby, brutalized surfaces of Cranach's flesh are not only broader than Dürer's, but they suggest an image hewn rather than simply printed from wood. Not surprisingly, Cranach's graphic language is far less dependent than Dürer's upon hatching and cross-hatching, that is, upon tonal gradations built up of small graphic units. But where they do appear, Cranach's are every bit as disciplined, often straighter, thicker, and more mechanical than Dürer's. Such contrasts of exuberant energy and rigid control inform Cranach's entire woodcut.

A similar dynamic characterizes Hans Baldung Grien's Saint Christopher of 1511–13. Obviously influenced by the rationality and precise cutting of Dürer's blocks of 1510 and 1511, it carries rigid control to the point of mannerism, transforming the ordered into the obsessive and irrational. The steely, wire-like lines contrast with the deep, crisply defined blacks of the uncut surface of the block and transform the gentle saint of safe passage and assurance against sudden death into a monumental image of intransigent resolve. Even the manner in which the sharply cut wood bites into the literal surface and figurative space of the paper evokes feelings of power and control. During the 1510s, Baldung's experiments with different types of cutting were nearly unique. Unlike the Saint Christopher, many of his woodcuts presented coarsely modeled, uneven tones; a Martyrdom of Saint Sebastian of 1514 achieves almost painterly effects with the mottled tones of its flickering surface.

By contrast, Hans Weiditz's Pietà of ca. 1515 almost evokes an attempt to transfer a brush drawing to wood. Indebted to Dürer's earliest *Apocalypse* woodcuts and perhaps self-consciously reverting to conventions of mid-fifteenth-century cutting—especially in the angular and splintered drapery folds—this is the only print I know of that found an equivalent for the poignant mixture of grief and beauty characteristic of the great sculpted Pietàs (*schönen Vesperbilder*) of 1380–1430. Executed with unusually broad means, the passages of hatched shadows, the delineation of muscles and ligaments, and the drawing of every limb and extremity coalesce into the moving drama of the Virgin's intimate embrace of the whole of the body of her son.

On the other end of the woodcut spectrum are Albrecht Altdorfer's masterpieces of the same decade. Modest to diminutive in size and executed in fine detail, these images succeed in awing their viewers with the gravity of their narratives and the vastness of their natural surroundings. Some of Altdorfer's works are very much like sparse pen-and-ink drawings, while others, such as his Saint Jerome in his Cell of 1518, are tonal masterpieces of extraordinary subtlety that exceeded anything imagined by Dürer. Complex systems of thread-fine hatchings evoke the mysterious, flickering shadows of Jerome's rocky grotto and suggest the scholarly isolation and dedication of the saint while simultaneously reminding the viewer of the modest scale of human accomplishment in the vast scheme of God's universe. Some of the same preoccupation with detail informed the work of Hans Burgkmair and the Augsburg cutters employed to complete several ambitious projects for Holy Roman Emperor Maximilian I, including the *Weisskunig,* an account of the Emperor's education and his military and political conquests (1514–16). Many of the artists mentioned above, including Dürer and Altdorfer, were contributors to these undertakings, but most of their designs were transformed by the more courtly but mechanical language of the Augsburg workshop. While that workshop's technical praxis derived from the best of Dürer's 1511 woodcuts, the Augsburg cutters (responsible for several hundred blocks) were more interested in layers of decorative surface effects than in sophisticated tonal effects, emotional expression, or narrative drama.

III.

The last section of this paper merely broaches the subject of the woodblocks themselves. While everyone knows that woodcuts were printed from blocks, there have been few studies devoted to those that survive.[13] There are several reasons for this. First and foremost, relatively few fifteenth-century and early sixteenth-century blocks still exist (aside from those associated with the Maximilian I projects). Second, the work of art—the artist's intention—resides in the print, not in the block. Third, blocks are notoriously difficult to photograph effectively, and even good photographs are very difficult to interpret. Whereas the print shows only the line (printed from the raised surface of the block), the block (or a photograph of one) shows the entire complex structure—lines, their sloping sides, and chiseled lower areas. What is blank white paper (optical space) in the print is the lowered wooden surface (physical material) of the block in the photograph. Thus when studying the sophisticated blocks of Dürer's time, it is extraordinarily difficult to separate visually the figure from the ground. Put another way, it is conceptually strenuous to imagine the process of cutting the wood while simultaneously focusing on the image that will emerge in the final print. This is not to mention the inevitable right-left reversal between block and print, to which it is relatively easy to accommodate. One can even—as I do in my lecture—reverse a slide of the block to conform with the print.

There is only one surviving block that is incontestably datable before the fourth quarter of the fifteenth century, the Martyrdom of Saint Sebastian of ca. 1470 in the Printroom of the British Museum.[14] By chance, a unique, fifteenth-century impression from this block exists in the collection of the Guildhall Library, London.[15] Shelley Fletcher and I believe that the technical execution of this block was typical of those executed during the third quarter of the century. The design consists almost entirely of contours, all of which stand up from the block (or, more accurately expressed, were cut down from the original surface) in pyramidal form, the crest of which carried the printer's ink. It took four cuts to disengage such a contour: two slanting cuts on each side to define it, and two more, begun at some remove and slanted in the opposite direction, to free the wood (and thus the line) from the first cuts. Most of the approximately two dozen blocks we have assigned to the years before 1490 manifest lines that are up to five millimeters in height, to ensure that the paper would not contact the residual lowered surfaces and pick up any ink that may have collected there. Sebastian's rounded rib cage and forearm contours were formed precisely in this manner. The few passages of hatching, which barely suggest either volume or shading, were often executed as collective units, both conceptually as a function of graphic coherence and physically as a means to provide maximum mutual support. Note, too, how Sebastian's right hand and arrow are joined in the block, again in an attempt to avoid leaving lines standing alone or allowing the paper to be torn or deformed between the ends of two lines.

It is crucial to understand that at this time, artist and cutter were very often two different individuals. It was the cutter's task to faithfully follow the drawing on the block. Judging from the present block, one could argue that the skill of the craftsman often outstripped the talents of the draftsman. This is certainly true in the case of the text, which was cut into the block just like the image. It offers support for the division of labor just proposed, as it is unlikely that a painter/draftsman would have concerned himself with the highly specialized procedure of cutting text. A similar argument can be made for the one surviving block from the *Schatzbehalter,* which we have already mentioned as being designed in 1491 by Michael Wolgemut for Dürer's godfather, the printer Anton Koberger. Its technique achieved a kind of shorthand for a style of rapid pen-and-ink drawing with limited spatial ambitions. The cutting itself is considerably shallower than that of the Saint Sebastian block, especially in areas of repeated hatchings, but the craft is essentially unchanged, simply more complicated. A basic vocabulary of curved and straight lines, often with angular meetings or twists, are neatly cut into the block. Despite the vast increase in the quantity of lines, the results are disappointingly limited in their abilities to model form, describe textures, and suggest light and local tone. Hatching appears in banks of straight parallels, neatly cut and cohesive; yet it does not achieve a convincing optical vibrancy because it fails to activate the intervening whites of the paper, which would generate the effect of tone and illuminated shadow. Many areas end up as confusing masses of line not unlike the jumbled and additive composition of human figures.[16] Nevertheless, it should be noted that by 1491 there was no lack of sophisticated and beautifully drawn woodcuts for printed books, especially those produced in Augsburg, Ulm, Mainz, and Lubeck (not to mention Florence and

Venice). But it was in the Wolgemut-Koberger productions of Nuremberg that the process of transforming the woodcut into a pictorial and tonal medium was initiated. It was this ambition that the young Albrecht Dürer inherited when he returned home from Italy in 1495 and commenced publishing his own woodcuts.[17]

Dürer's block for the Martyrdom of the Ten Thousand belongs to the British Museum. Aside from the profound influence of Italian draftsmanship, it is the reclamation of space that contrasts so strikingly with the filled surface of the *Schatzbehalter* block.[18] Line is finer, more malleable, curvilinear, and descriptive; contours not only move through space but are often formed by the open edges of groups of hatchings, as is evident in the bound nude in the center of the composition. The wood is cut with an impressive variety of shapes and hatchings, all consciously permeated by an awareness of the white of the paper. While not quite evoking sensations of light and atmosphere, the image is filled with a completely new evocation of shimmering textures and materials alive with optical variability. Nearly every cut line has its own dynamic life but acts in concert with its neighbors, activating the whole surface. This new airiness and graphic order, the descending columns of scalloped hatchings that sculpt both the block and the space it represents, and the presence of occasional broken, reversing, angular lines between passages of curvilinear hatching are very much a translation of Dürer's drawing style of the mid-1490s, such as the pen drawings for the stained-glass Life of Saint Benedict.

Another early Dürer block, Hercules Killing Cacus, also belongs to the British Museum.[19] Here the influence of Andrea Mantegna is unmistakable in the figure types and the decorative flair of the clinging antique draperies as well as in the choice of a classical subject rendered with the tightly controlled vocabulary of highly emotive gestures. Cascades of flowing drapery and systems of repeated hatching add to the spatial dynamics of the image, which in the block read almost as if they were modeled in low relief rather than a perfectly flat surface (all printing lines stand at the same height). Despite that claim, some lines, like the hatchings that model the neck, arm, and face of the avenging fury pursuing Cacus' sister, run down into the lowered surface of the block. Some have proposed that this was intended to introduce a feathering of such shaded passages, but I would contend that it was a common device to protect the lines from breaking during printing.[20] Such a device also added to the sense of unity that was gradually instilled into Dürer's blocks—the measured expressiveness of the figures and the controlled precision of the hatching. Cutter and artist have again raised the technique of cutting to new levels of skill and insight. Series of changeable, tightly curved lines, which in the print interact with the white of the paper to form rounded surfaces and volumes, pulse with an inner volition, as in Hercules' arms and legs.[21] Unfortunately

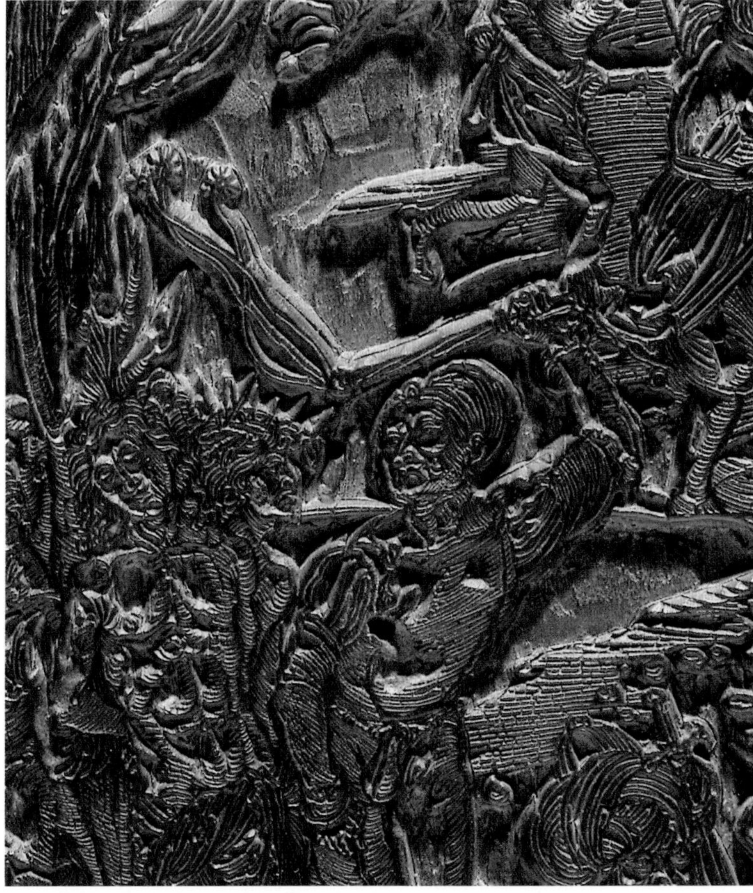

Fig. 8. Albrecht Dürer. Martyrdom of the Ten Thousand, detail of original woodblock, 1496–97 (British Museum, London). See Fig. 3 for woodcut.

none of the contemporary blocks for the *Apocalypse* or the *Large Passion* survive, so it is impossible to follow in wood the developments that are so obvious on paper.

The block for the Martyrdom of Saint Catherine, ca. 1498, must date toward the end of this first phase of major development. As usual, Dürer compressed more than a single event into one unified image: Catherine's martyrdom by both wheel and beheading. The composition, now even more compacted, consists of alternating lights and darks. In the same spirit, the draftsmanship shifts almost imperceptibly from passages that appear to be articulated by highlights and those that are shaped by shadows. Catherine and her executioner appear in relief, modeled by an unseen source of light to the right and by the shadows of the encroaching background to the left. As in the last prints of the *Apocalypse* and the 1498 prints from the *Large Passion*—the Woman

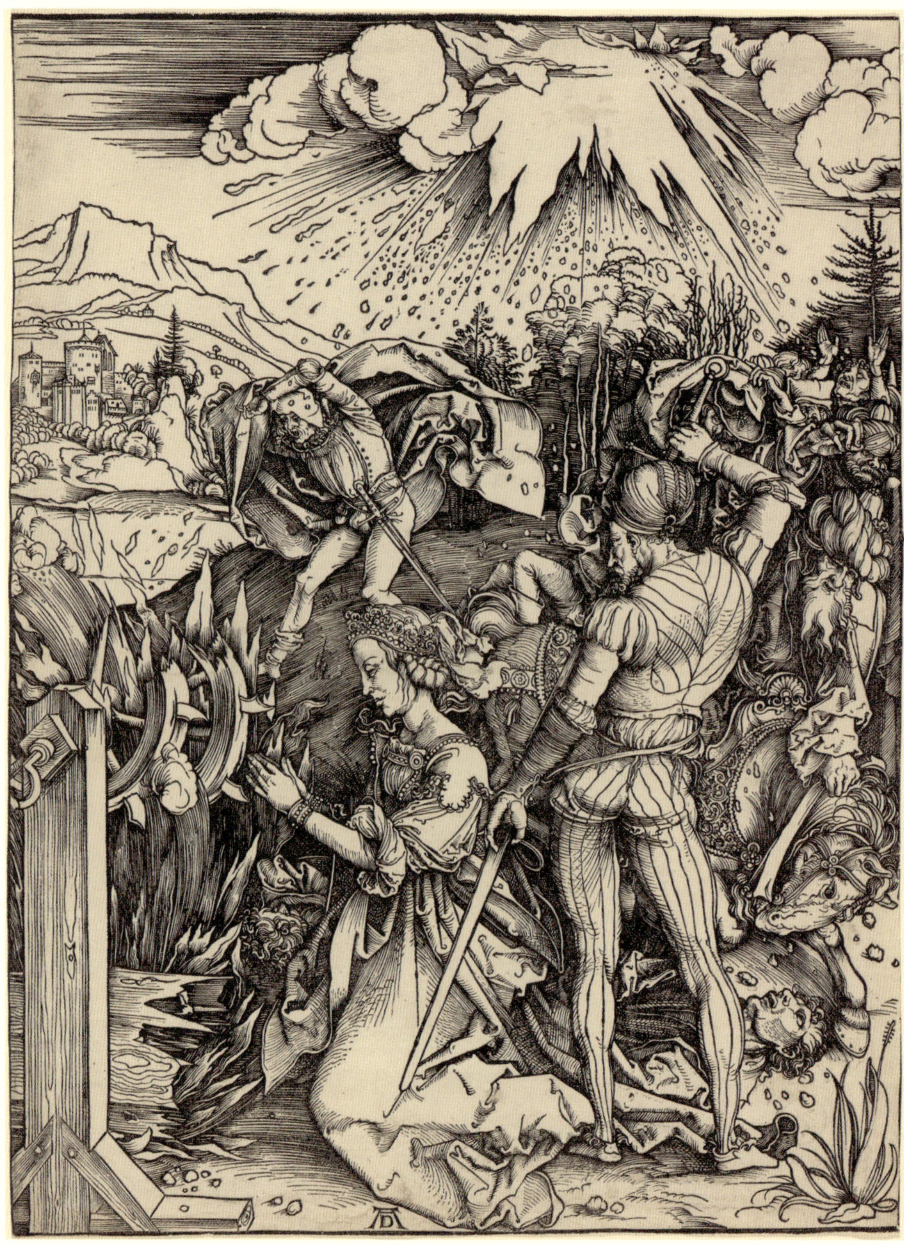

Fig. 9. Albrecht Dürer. Martyrdom of Saint Catherine, woodcut, ca. 1498 (Rosenwald Collection, National Gallery of Art. © Board of Trustees, National Gallery of Art, Washington).

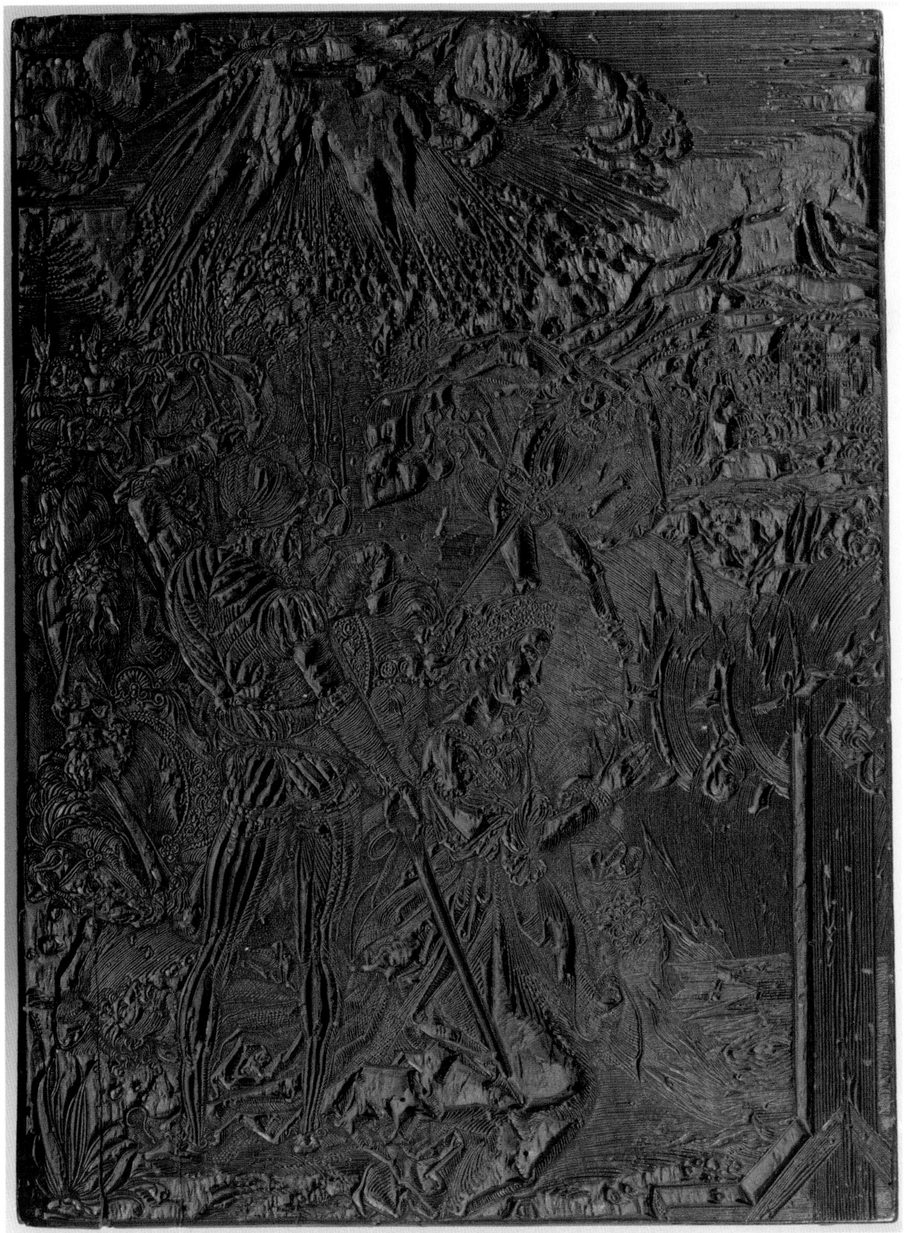

Fig. 10. Albrecht Dürer. Martyrdom of Saint Catherine, original woodblock ca. 1498 (The Metropolitan Museum of Art, Gift of Junius S. Morgan, 1919. 19.73.256. Image © The Metropolitan Museum of Art).

Clothed in the Sun, the Martyrdom of Saint John, the Lamentation, and the Bearing of the Cross—both the block and the print reveal an overall decorative sense and a further unification of surface. Such calligraphic impulses inform the dense and variable sculpted hatchings of Catherine's head, while the deep shadow area behind her neck consists of subtle cuts that barely intrude upon the original surface of the block. This new emphasis on surface cutting foretells of future developments in Dürer's blocks.

Unfortunately there are again significant lacunae among the remaining blocks; none survive from the *Life of the Virgin*, seventeen of which were executed from 1502 to 1505.[22] On the other hand, thirty-five of the thirty-seven blocks for the *Small Woodcut Passion* (1508–10) do exist.[23] Few if any scholars suggest that Dürer cut this series of blocks, since there is considerable internal evidence that several different craftsmen were employed in their execution.[24] Comparison of the rather worn block for the Entombment with a brilliant, early impression quickly manifests its subtle and miniaturized cutting. Most of the major elements of the design are now conceived as being cut "against" an abstract tonal ground. In the restricted format of each block Dürer realized a tonally coherent design, compressing figure and ground into the surface plane. Enormous discipline is also evident in passages such as the uniformly scalloped hatchings, which descend like the splayed slices of fruit in a French apple peach tart. Such precise control was demanded by the desire to create graphic passages whose function was primarily pictorial and secondarily delineation or description.

When one looks back over the woodcuts of 1496–1509, it becomes clear that Dürer only gradually initiated and achieved his quest to illuminate his subjects and subsequently to articulate entire compositions through the sensation of light. This probably made greater demands upon the cutters' skills than did the artist's variegated, calligraphic contours. Not only did it require precise control over the spacing and form of contiguous lines, but, more crucially, it required a knowledge of how individual tonal passages would merge and harmonize with those of the whole block. These new conditions force a reframing of the question of whether Dürer cut his own blocks. Were his ambitions fulfilled by profound changes in cutting techniques or simply by following the increasing demands of his original drawings on the blocks? My tentative formulation is that Dürer's vision changed the cutter's *conceptual* approach to the woodcut radically, but his *physical* approach to cutting only modestly. The skills of the cutter were formidably challenged, but not substantively changed. First and foremost, as already stated, lines had to be freed in a very cumbersome manner to print black ink; there is no reason to believe that this basic skill did not form the basis for cutting Dürer's blocks. Only occasionally, for example, did Dürer use "white" lines, and for the most part early in his experiments in woodcut; when they did appear (in Men's

Bath, Martyrdom of Saint Catherine), they were largely confined to articulating spatial displacements in the region of contours. He never seems to have suggested the use of the burin to excise white lines from the wood.[25] There were, however, two remarkable innovations that sharpened and transformed these existing cutting skills. First, the emergence of banks of fine, curvilinear, tonal hatching required subtle innovations to assure that such lines would resist breaking down under the pressure of printing (the French tart model); in essence, such passages became self-supporting. And second, the wish to create delicate patterns, porous textures, gleaming highlights, and illuminated shadows accelerated the trend toward shallower cutting in areas of great detail and subtle tone. Whole sections of the block might be cut to a depth of only one millimeter. Although the same knives and skills were employed, the conceptual thinking had undergone a change, from one that regarded the work as primarily linear to one that focused on tone, on groups of marks that collectively and simultaneously summoned up impressions of light, texture, and depth.

The pinnacle of perfection, reached in 1511, can be viewed in the large single woodcut of the Resurrection (the block for which no longer exists). Here, the pictorial synthesis that had begun in the blocks of the *Small Passion* and in the last (1510) blocks of the *Large Passion* reaches its apotheosis in a completely integrated and organic whole. Such overarching unity could only be provided by the new, abstract systems of cutting. There is no imitation and little "analog" cutting. It is all "digital," all a function of light and shade that create an illusion of line, shape, form, surface, texture, modeling, light, and luminous shadow.

But this synthesis could not hold. In the years subsequent to 1511 it gave rise to numerous variations, including those fashioned by Dürer and his collaborators. One was a very decorative technique of cutting, which Dürer and his cutter, Hieronymus Andreae, worked out in the commissions they received from Maximilian I, first in their contributions to the *Small Triumphal Chariot* of 1516–18.[26] The courtly, calligraphic style was remarkably open and linear, quite devoid of passages of tonal cross-hatching that characterized the works of 1508–11. Dürer contributed to other projects for Maximilian I, and these were executed in a somewhat different and drier manner by a group of cutters in Augsburg, presumably under the supervision of artist Hans Burgkmair and *Formschneider* Jost de Nekar. Typical of the flat, surface-style of execution is a block from the unpublished Freydal, The Masquerade: Dance by Torch Light, 1517–18.[27] The highly skillful imposition of lace-like draftsmanship "over" a ground of abstract, tonal hatching pales in comparison with Dürer's 1508–11 accomplishments. Yet the several hundred blocks for the Maximilian projects were among the most accomplished in the annals of professional block cutting. Most are preserved in the Graphische Sammlung in Albertina, Vienna.

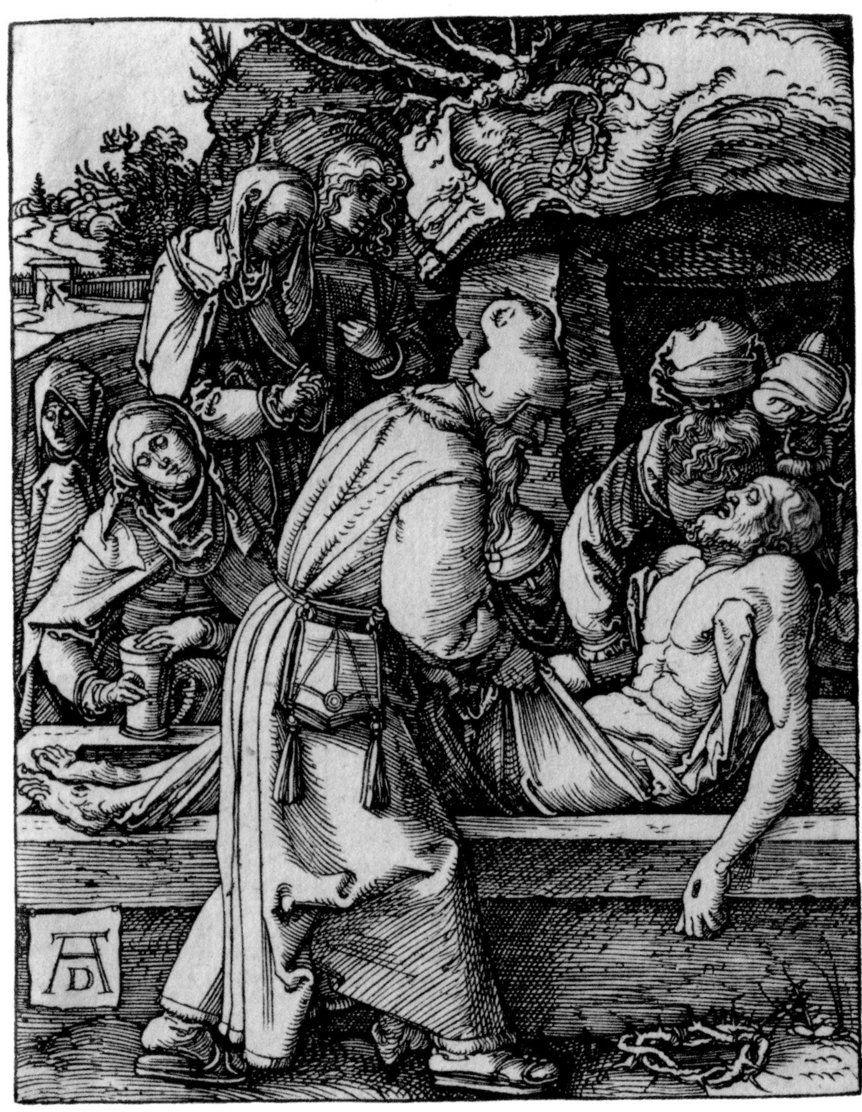

Fig. 11. Albrecht Dürer. Entombment, woodcut from the *Small Passion*, 1508–10 (Rosenwald Collection, National Gallery of Art. © Board of Trustees, National Gallery of Art, Washington).

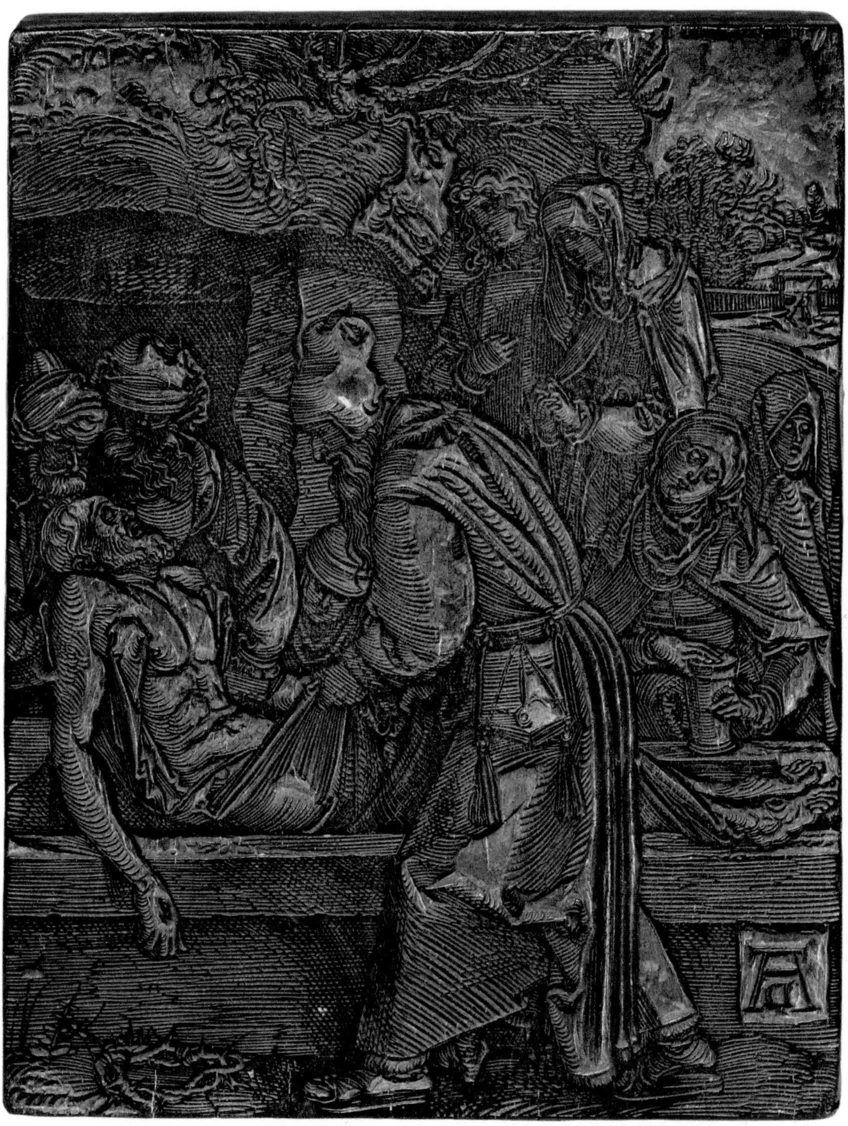

Fig. 12. Albrecht Dürer. Entombment, original woodblock from the *Small Passion*, 1508–10 (British Museum, London).

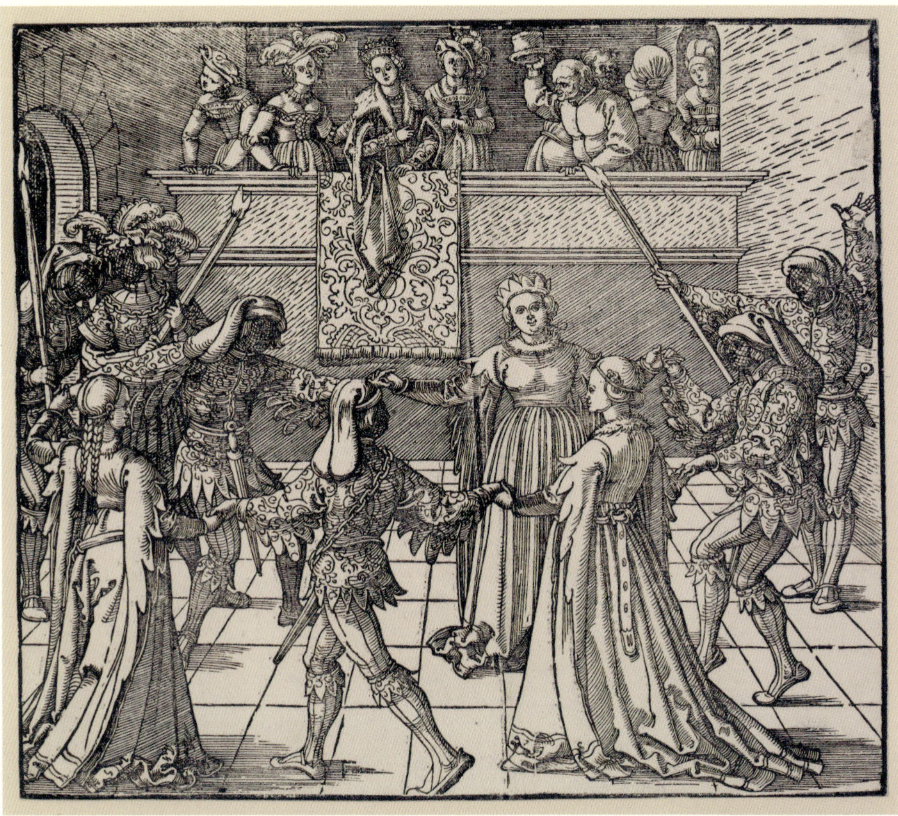

Fig. 13. Albrecht Dürer. The Masquerade: Dance by Torch Light, woodcut for *Freydal*, 1517–18 (Dodgson 1903, No. 135, British Museum, London).

Whether Dürer cut his own blocks is a question that has occasioned considerable debate since the late eighteenth century. In support of Dürer's responsibility for the pre-1500 blocks were Christoph von Murr and Johann Gottlob Breitkopf. Their claims, however, were quickly disputed by Adam von Bartsch, who was a staunch supporter of the separation between art and craft.[28] It is a quandary we are unable to fully address at this time, but a sensible solution seems at hand. We do not know to what extent Dürer was trained to cut blocks. Certainly his exposure to the craft both in Koberger's printing establishment and Wolgemut's workshop, his early book illustrations, and his lifelong romance with the medium vouch for his extraordinary interest in the woodcut. Even if we assume that there is no credible evidence that he carved any of the blocks published in Basel and Strasbourg during his *Wanderjahre* of the early 1490s, the innovations after 1496 are so striking that he must have been

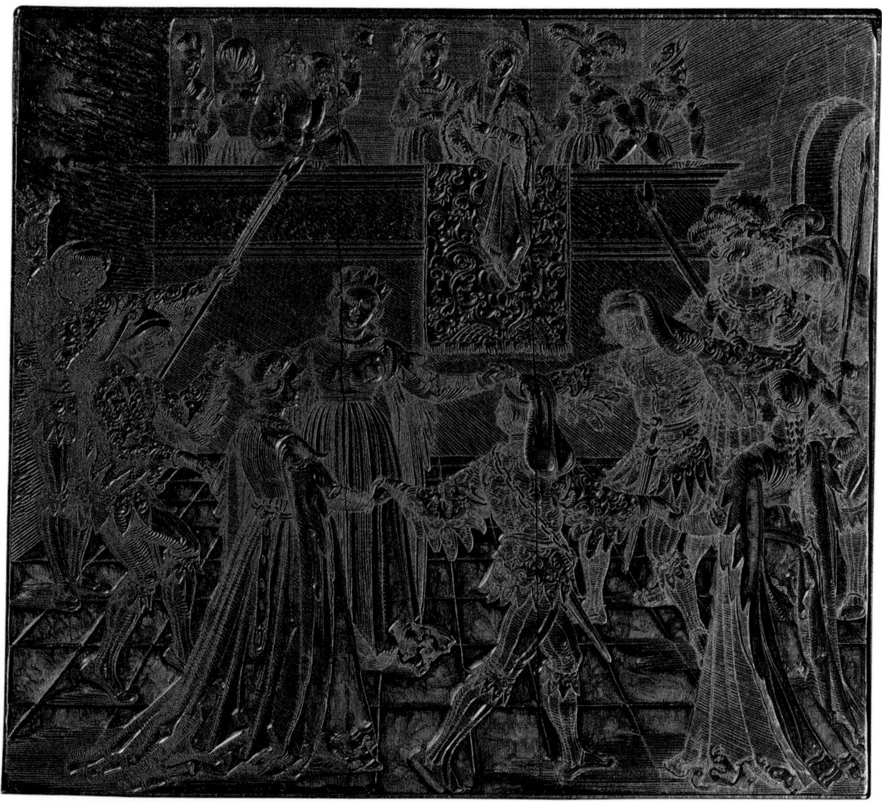

Fig. 14. Albrecht Dürer. The Masquerade: Dance by Torch Light, original block for *Freydal* (Bildarchiv Preussischer Kulturbesitz / Art Resource, NY).

more than a mere designer. One could make a strong case that Dürer followed the accepted practice of his day, namely that he insisted that cutters adapt their skills to his pen-and-ink drawings, thereby revolutionizing the medium. But the blocks manifest so much experimentation and change, such a constant working toward a synthesis of medieval and Renaissance modes of vision, that Dürer must have played more than such a passive role in their execution. I believe he collaborated with the best cutters in Nuremberg, possibly taking up the knife himself to assist in refining the techniques appropriate to his graphic vision. On the other hand, I doubt that Dürer went so far as to assume total responsibility for the cutting of his own blocks. The professional skills existed and only needed to be reformed and raised to higher levels of sophistication. In my opinion, William M. Ivins, Jr. was wrong to attach so much significance to refinements like series of hatchings that curved down into the block. Yes, Dürer's blocks show an increasing use of this method of self-reinforcement, but such a refinement was the hallmark of the professional cutter, and it began to emerge in earlier blocks. Moreover, I have not been able to confirm Ivins' additional contention that certain lines were carefully lowered in order to affect nuances in the printing of blacks. Within very close tolerances, all lines designed to print are of the same height. What the master forced on his cutters were ways of shaping lines, of making them dynamic, of countless means of achieving textures, but principally, how to organize the surface, how to make the woodcut into a fully rationalized tonal image governed by light and shade and nuanced by illuminated shadows. Collaboration has always been suspect for the historian and the public alike. It runs counter to the notions of individual innovation and creative genius that have shaped much of our admiration for the giants of printmaking. The influence of craftsmen has perpetually been undervalued. Even today, when collaboration of every conceivable kind has accounted for the very best in printmaking, there remains a residue of resistance. Yet collaboration is one of the worthy lessons of our time, and I believe it is the most sane and human solution to what is an otherwise unsolvable problem. It may well have been the path taken by another early Renaissance master, Andrea Mantegna, whose engravings, from the moment of their appearance in the third quarter of the fifteenth century, were astonishingly original and masterful. In Dürer's case, the artist guided the cutter's conception; in Mantegna's, the engraver guided the artist's hand.[29]

NOTES

1. Schreiber 285m. See Wilhelm Ludwig Schreiber, *Handbuch der Holz- und Metallschnitte des fünfzehnten Jahrhunderts* (Leipzig: Hiersemann, 1926–30). This brief generalization overlooks the exceptional draftsmanship of Netherlandish blockbooks and Venetian woodcuts of 1450–70.

2. This term is borrowed from Hans Körner, *Der früheste deutsche Einblattholzschnitt,* eds. Hermann Bauer and Friedrich Piel, Studia Iconologia 3 (Mittenwald: Mäander, 1979), 65–66.

3. Erwin Panofsky, *The Life and Art of Albrecht Dürer* (Princeton: Princeton University Press, 1955), 18–21, 44–62. These few pages contain what is certainly the most insightful writing on woodcuts of any period. Even the most recent tome on Dürer's woodcuts, Rainer Schoch, Matthias Mende, and Anna Scherbaum, et al., *Albrecht Dürer—Das druckgraphische Werk, Vol. 2, Holzschnitte und Holzschnittfolgen* (Munich: Prestel, 2002), offers little to amplify or surpass Panofsky's formulations and descriptions of the development of Dürer's woodcut technique. The Meder numbers used in the present article are from Josef Meder, *Dürer-Katalog. Ein Handbuch über Albrecht Dürers Stiche, Radierungen, Holzschnitte*... (Vienna: Gilhofer & Ranschburg, 1932).

4. See Schoch, Mende, Scherbaum, et al. (cited note 3), 44.

5. Although of another order of brilliance, one has to mention the great *Apocalypse* blockbook executed in the southern Netherlands around 1450. See *Blockbücher des Mittelalters: Bilderfolgen als Lektüre,* exh. cat. (Mainz: Gutenberg Gesellschaft and Gutenberg-Museum, 1991), 59–119. The draftsmanship of the first edition, while attempting none of the pictorial descriptiveness of Dürer's work (which came almost five decades later), is among the most sophisticated examples of drawing in wood of the entire century. Its line, and it is particularly linear, combines both the flowing grace of curvilinear contours and the natural jagged planarity of the wood surface from which it is extricated.

6. One of these cutters, Sebald Gallensdorfer, is known from his work on the unpublished *Archetypus triumphantus Romae* (c. 1493–96). See Rainer Schoch, "'Archetypus triumphantis Romae,' Zu einem gescheiterten Buchprojekt des Nürnberger Frühumanismus," in *50 Jahre Sammler und Mäzen: Der Historische Verein Schweinfurt seinem Ehrenmitglied Otto Schäfer (1912–2000) zum Gedenken,* Veröffentlichungen des Historischen Vereins Schweinfurt, e.V. (Schweinfurt: 2001), 261–98.

7. It has never been definitively decided which figure represents the Virgin and which Mary Magdalene.

8. The *Life of the Virgin,* executed from 1503 to 1506 (Meder 188–207), concluded with two works from 1510. It was mostly concerned with continuing the volumetric and spatial features of the previous years, often with stately compositions in bold architectural settings. While they abandoned much of the Late Gothic emotionalism and elaboration of the earlier woodcuts in favor of composed Renaissance compositions, they appear as charming way stations on the path to the radical revisions that culminated in 1510. The eleven "*schlecte Holzwerk,*" executed from 1503 to 1505 (Meder 180, 213, 214, 221, 222, 224, 225, 230, 233, 235, and 237), on the other hand, raise many interesting problems that also cannot be dealt with here. Chief among them is exactly how to account for the loss in quality and sophistication even in the more human, humbler presentation of holy figures. If we assume, as all scholars have, that they were drawn by Dürer, could the designs have been transferred by a lesser hand or cut in wood by a less gifted *Formschneider?* Or were they actually intended by the artist to be a grade rougher, heavier, and simpler, both in technique and in draftsmanship?

9. Panofsky also emphasizes the Italian (Venetian) roots of the three-tone system. It derives from a manner of drawing in black and white chalks on prepared (most often blue) papers. The tone of the paper acts as the neutral gray, while the chalks act both as drawing and as highlights and shadows.

10. See Wilhelm Worringer, *Abstraction and Empathy: A Contribution to the Psychology of Style,* trans. Michael Bullock (New York: International Universities Press, 1967. 2nd ed., Chicago: Ivan R. Dee, 1997); Jacquelynn Baas and Richard S. Field, *The Artistic Revival of the Woodcut in France 1850–1900,* exh. cat. (Ann Arbor: The University of Michigan Museum of Art, 1984); Rainer Schoch, "Lost in the Wood: The Early Woodcut and the Artistic

Avant-Garde, 1890–1980," in *Origins of European Printmaking: Fifteenth-Century Woodcuts and Their Public,* ed. Peter Parshall and Rainer Schoch, exh. cat. (Washington, DC: National Gallery of Art, 2005), 7–13.

11. But what might a reassignment to "Dürer school" mean? That the image was not drawn (designed) by Dürer? That he did not draw directly on the block, and that the image was transferred by an assistant or specialist? That his most talented cutter did not execute the block? That Dürer did not cut the block himself? Or even that the entire production came from another workshop, simply lifting the master's style? This debate cannot be resolved. In entry 228 of Schoch, Mende, Scherbaum catalogue (see note 3), Yasmin Doosry reproduces the verso of an impression of this 1511 *Saint Christopher* (Meder 223, Hessisches Landesmuseum, Darmstadt). This verso shows a ghostly offset from a moist impression of a completely accepted Dürer woodcut, the small *Death of Abel,* also dated 1511 (Meder 106). As a consequence one may justifiably conclude that both woodcuts were produced in Dürer's workshop, but the question of authorship is still not completely resolved. Since there have been few who have doubted the ultimate design was the master's, the woodcut could be regarded as a later equivalent of the "*schlecte Holzwerk,*" that is, as perfectly genuine but less ambitious. Certainly none of the blocks for the post-1500 woodcuts were cut by Dürer, so that is not the issue. Furthermore, I do not believe we can decide whether the artist drew on the block. In my opinion, the wisest and most fruitful solution is to accept the woodcut as being Dürer's and to regard it as exemplary for the future of the medium (along with two other *Holy Families* and the large *Christ on the Cross* of 1513, Meder 215, 216, 182).

12. See David Rosand and Michelangelo Muraro, *Titian and the Venetian Woodcut,* exh. cat. (Washington, DC: International Exhibitions Foundation, 1976–77).

13. Hans Albrecht, Freiherr von Derschau, *Holzschnitte alter deutscher Meister in den Originalplatten gesammelt von Hans Albrech von Derschau / als ein Beytrag zur Kunstgeschichte hrsg. Und mit einer Abhandlung über die Holzschneidekunst und deren Schicksale von Rudolph Zacharias Becker,* 3 vols. (Gotha: L'éditeur, 1808–16); Ernst Holzinger, "Hat Dürer den Basler Hieronymus von 1492 selbst geschnitten?" *Mittheilungen der Gesellschaft für vervielfältigende Kunst* 51 (1928): 17–21; William M. Ivins, Jr., "Notes on Three Dürer Woodblocks," *Metropolitan Museum Studies* 2 (1929–30): 102–11; Franz Winzinger, "Albrecht Altdorfers Münchner Holzstock," *Jahrbuch der bildenden Kunst,* 3rd series, 1 (1950): 191–203; Klaus-Dieter Jäger and Renate Kroll, "Holzanatomische Untersuchungen an den Altdorfen-Stöcken der Sammlung Derschau: Ein Beitrag zur Methodik von Holzbestimmungen an Kunstgegenständen," *Forschung und Berichte, Staatliche Museen zu Berlin* 6 (1964): 24–39.

14. Another convincing block, probably a decade or two earlier, belongs to the Württemburgisches Landesmuseum, Stuttgart. It is also a double-sided block with a *Nativity* (Schreiber 62) and a *Christ on the Mount of Olives* (Schreiber 186). 276 × 420 × 21 mm. See H. Theodore Musper, "Ein früher Holzstock in Stuttgart," *Zeitschrift für bildende Kunst* 64 (1930–31): 7–9. Unfortunately no early impressions from this block exist.

15. Schreiber 1678. These are are more fully discussed in the catalogue of the exhibition *Origins of European Printmaking* (see note 10), cat. nos. 4 and 5. The verso of this woodblock also bears an image, the *Monogram of Christ* (Schreiber 1812).

16. In this case it is not at all clear whether the shortcomings of the resulting woodcut reflect those of the draftsman or of the cutter (if not both). It cannot be assumed that the designs for the *Schatzbehalter* blocks were from a single hand (Wolgemut) any more than that they were cut by a single cutter.

17. On Dürer's early book illustrations, see Schoch, Mende, Scherbaum, *Albrecht Dürer—Das druckgraphische Werk,* vol. 3: *Buchillustration* (Munich: Prestel, 2004).

18. The many influences of Italian art on Dürer's work are amply discussed in Panofsky; Schoch, Mende, Scherbaum; and throughout the Dürer literature.

19. For another title and source for this image see Simon's and Mesenzeva's separate essays of 1971, cited in Schoch, Mende, Scherbaum (note 3), entry 105.

20. See Ivins, "Notes on Three Dürer Woodblocks," (see note 13). Ivins was the very first to observe these nuances of carving. He was convinced that they were Dürer's own innovations, but their beginnings in earlier blocks like the Feltenstein and Archetypus blocks are mentioned in *Origins of European Printmaking* (see note 10), cat. 4, 6, 7.

21. This block is exceptionally difficult to read, even when accompanied by a good impression; the block seems so much more complex and busy, while the print seems to be composed of so much blank white space. One wonders whether this discrepancy was not consciously addressed in the gradual simplification of subsequent blocks.

22. Meder 188–207. It is interesting to observe that in this series Dürer appears to move again from complexity toward simplicity in both style and technique. Of course, this judgment is based on the general consensus of how the series is to be ordered, which may in itself incorporate such a bias.

23. Meder 125–162.

24. See Sir Henry Cole, *The Passion of our Lord Jesus Christ* (London: Cundall, 1844), preface. According to Cole, the wood engraver John Thompson (1785–1866) claimed to have discerned four cutters at work on these blocks. While he gave examples of the four hands, nowhere did he attempt to describe the differences he perceived among the blocks. See also Campbell Dodgson, *Catalogue of Early German and Flemish Woodcuts preserved in the Department of Prints and Drawings in the British Museum,* vol. 1 (London: British Museum, 1903), 293–97; and for interesting observations about the actual sawing of the pearwood blocks, see Giulia Bartrum, *German Renaissance Prints 1490–1550,* exh. cat. (London: British Museum, 1995), cat. no. 28. Americans would describe most of these blocks as having been "quarter sawn."

25. "White" lines are the absence of pigment in the print, but they are formed by the surrounding printed blacks. As opposed to the knife, which requires two strokes to define the edges of a white line, the burin creates white lines with completely parallel sides. The reciprocal nature of black and white can make it difficult to distinguish line from ground, but not often in the work of Dürer and his contemporaries. It is almost as if the burin, the engraver's tool used to remove lines from his copper plate, were forbidden to the woodcutter either by regulation or by praxis. During our observations of various early blocks, Shelley Fletcher, formerly Chief Paper Conservator at the National Gallery, Washington, and I have often discussed the employment of the burin, but in almost no instances have we both been convinced that it had been used. In his last great woodcut, the *Last Supper* of 1518 (Meder 184), Dürer completely avoided white lines.

26. Meder 253. Only the two first blocks of the entire procession (of 137) were designed by Dürer. One of these (the *Horse-drawn Wagon with Victory*) is now in the Graphische Sammlung Albertina, Vienna. See Schoch, Mende, Scherbaum 2002, no. 239.

27. Meder 250. Along with the *Theuerdank* and the *Weißkunig,* these books were dedicated to documenting the youth and education, as well as the political, social, and military deeds of the Emperor. See Campbell Dodgson, "Die Freydal-Holzschnitte Dürers," *Repertorium für Kunstwissenschaft* 25 (1902): 447–49.

28. For example, see Christoph G. von Murr, "Beweiss, daß Albrecht Dürer selbst in Holz geschnitten habe," *Journal zur Kunstgeschichte und zur allgemein Literatur,* 9 (1780): 52–55; Johann Gottlob Immanuel Breitkopf, *Versuch, den ursprung der spielkarten, die einführung des leinenpapieres, und den anfang der holzschneidekunst in Europa zu erforschen* (Leipzig: the Author, 1784–1801); Adam von Bartsch, *Le Peintre-Graveur,* vol. 7 (Vienna: J. V. Degen, 1808), 12–24; C. Fr. von Rumohr, *Zur Geschichte und Theorie der Formschneidekunst* (Leipzig: Anstalt für Kunst und Literatur, 1837), 7ff.

29. See the opposing views of David Landau: "Mantegna as Printmaker," in *Andrea Mantegna,* exh. cat. (London: Royal Academy of Arts and New York: The Metropolitan Museum of Art, 1992), 44–55; Suzanne Boorsch, "Mantegna and his Printmakers," in *Andrea Mantegna,* op. cit., 56–67; and Shelley Fletcher, "A Re-evaluation of Two Mantegna Prints," *Print Quarterly* 14 (March 1997): 67–77.

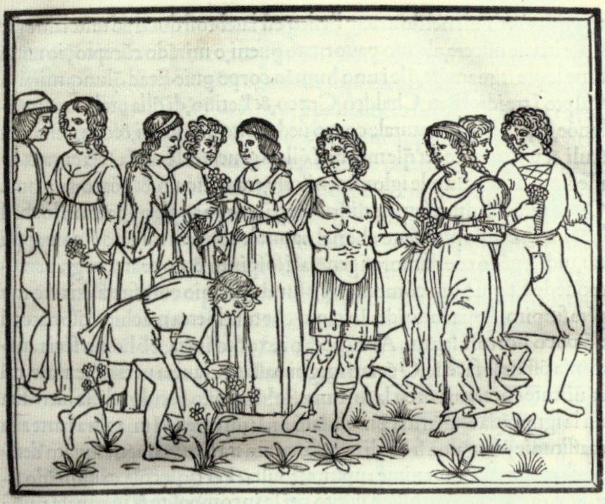

Stupefacto dunque non poco, ruminando, & cũ summo dilecto curioso riguardãdo tale ingente machina conflata in animale da humano ingenio, dignissimo imaginato. Che in omni membro indefectamente participasse la egregia harmonia & compaginatione. Onde nella retinente memoria mi soccorse il sfortuneuole cauallo Seiano.

Da poscia allucinato di tale artificioso mysterio offerẽtise nõ meno mirãdo spectaculo ad gliochii mei uno maxio Elephãto, cũ sũma uoluptate di ꝓpare ad qllo. Ma echo che io ĩ unaltra ꝑte sento uno ægritudiale gemito humão. Io alhora ĩcõtinẽte steti, subleuati gli capigli, sẽza altro cõsulto, uerso il gemito festinãte, uno agere di ruine scãdo di grãde fracture & recisamẽti marmorei. Et ĩde accõciamẽte ꝓgresso. Echo chio uedo uno Vastissimo & mirãdo colosso, Cũ li pedi senza solea excauati & tutte le Tibie peruie & uacue. Et dĩdi al capo cũ horrore ĩspectabõdo uenẽdo, Cõiectu rai che laura ĩtromessa ꝑ le patorate piãte, cũ diuino ĩuento, il gemito moderatamẽte expsso causaua. Ilq̃le iaceua decũbẽdo supino di metallo mirabile artificio cõflato, di media ætate, subleuato alquãto sopra uno puluino tenẽdo il capo. Cũ sembiãte di ægro, cũ la bucca di suspirare & gemere ĩdicãte. hiãte, di ꝓceritate passi.60. Et ꝑ li crini sopra il pecto se poteua ascẽdere, Et ꝑ li tomẽtati & tormẽtati pili dilla fulta barba, alla lamẽtabonda bucca. Ilq̃le meato samẽte era tutto ianc & uacuo. Per qlla dũq; dal curioso scrutario stimulo, sẽza altro cõsultamine ĩpulso, nella gula ꝑ graduli ĩ-

Lilian Armstrong

Woodcuts in Classical Texts Printed in Venice, 1490–1520, and the Role of Benedetto Bordon as a Designer

Miniaturists and Woodcut Design, 1490s–1500

For anyone interested in Venetian Renaissance painting, the period from 1490 to 1520 is an extraordinary one. Giovanni Bellini (c. 1430–1516) was the great artist of the older generation who continued to paint masterpiece after masterpiece until his death in 1516, including *The Feast of the Gods* of 1513, now in the National Gallery of Art in Washington. Giogione's innovations dominated Venetian painting from 1500 to 1510, for example, the new vision of landscape found in his famous *Tempesta*. By 1520, Titian had completed magnificent secular and religious paintings such as the *Sacred and Profane Love* of 1512 and the *Assumption of the Virgin* of 1519.[1] Given the stupendous achievements of these artists, it is perhaps not surprising that art historians have paid much less attention to the woodcuts in Venetian books of this same period.

It should be recognized, however, that an extraordinary repository of visual images exists in the manuscripts and printed books created in Venice between 1490 and 1520. In the catalogue of the *Heavenly Craft* exhibition, I discussed woodcuts in liturgical books printed in Venice around 1500, and there I argued that the distinguished miniaturist Benedetto Bordon was the designer of some important sequences of these religious woodcuts.[2] A telling comparison can be made between a miniature painted by Bordon in the late 1490s and a woodcut of the same subject, the Calling of Peter and Andrew, that was first printed by LucAntonio Giunta in a *Missale romanum* in 1501, and later reused in a *Breviarium romanum* of 1507, both now in the Rosenwald Collection

Fig. 1. Youths and Maidens Picking Flowers, woodcut in [Francesco Colonna], *Hypnerotomachia poliphili*, Venice, Aldus Manutius, 1499, fol. b6, woodcut design attributed to Benedetto Bordon (Wellesley, MA., Clapp Library, Special Collections, Wellesley College. *81W-5q.).

of the Library of Congress.[3] Bordon's miniature is characterized by figures in stately poses wearing brilliantly colored garments, set in a luminous landscape. Similar figures of the saints reappear in the woodcut, leaning toward Christ from their boat as it nears the shore. The image is now only black and white, the figures handsomely modeled to suggest their volumetric bodies.

In this paper, instead, I discuss woodcuts in classical texts, that is, texts by Greek and Latin authors. On the one hand, I want to evaluate whether or not some of the woodcuts in classical texts were also designed by Benedetto Bordon, as part of an ongoing effort to evaluate Bordon's importance to this significant moment in Venetian Renaissance art. But in a larger context, I survey the classical woodcuts broadly in order to understand more clearly the quantities and qualities of classical imagery available to artists and readers at this time.

The comparison of Bordon's miniature with the corresponding woodcut stands for a broader phenomenon. Artists who were trained as illuminators of manuscripts in Venice in the late fifteenth century lived into the age of printing. And from the very beginning of the industry these artists were employed in illuminating individual copies of printed books. These same illuminators were subsequently the first to design woodcuts, the art that would ultimately supersede manuscript illumination.

An example of this practice appears in a copy of a Pliny the Elder, *Historia naturalis* that was printed in an edition of over a thousand copies by Nicolaus Jenson in Venice in 1476. This particular copy, which was formerly in the William Foyle Collection, was turned over to a miniaturist who illuminated the margins of the opening page by painting a spectacular architectural border around the printed text.[4] He depicted the owner's coat of arms, a plethora of "all'antica" architectural motifs, and the imaginary portrait of the author in the space reserved for the incipit letter. The artist, who is known as the Pico Master, decorated dozens of printed books in this manner during the period 1469 to about 1490.

The Pliny frontispiece may be compared with that of another printed book, a Livy, *Historiae Romanae decades* (in Italian) printed in Venice in 1493.[5] Surrounding the text is an elaborate woodcut frame featuring many motifs that are similar to the painted Pliny frontispiece. The thin architectural components, the elongated and swaying putti, and almost fragile adult figures resemble similar features in the illuminated frontispiece of the 1476 Pliny, and they confirm that the Pico Master also designed the woodcut. The large woodcut above Livy's text represents ambassadors from Egypt before the Roman Senate; at the right, one returns to report to the King of Egypt. The two encounters are vividly composed, but the artist has made no effort to dress the Roman senators in classical garments. The Livy woodcut shows that by the early 1490s, the Pico Master, like Benedetto Bordon, understood that the art of hand-illumination was nearing its end, and he had adapted to a new art of woodcut design.

The provenance of the 1476 Pliny and the 1493 Livy link them to the *Heavenly Craft* exhibition. The beautiful Pliny was at one time in the Dyson Perrins collection, from which Lessing Rosenwald bought all of the books in the exhibition. A copy of the 1493 Livy is also in the Library of Congress, in the Lessing J. Rosenwald Collection which these symposium papers celebrate.[6]

Benedetto Bordon, the "Classical Designer" and the "Shaded Style"

IN 1935 ARTHUR M. HIND set out a broad outline of Venetian woodcuts in his *Introduction to a History of Woodcut* by identifying three overlapping stages of development.[7] Firstly, Hind noted the lively style of the 1493 Livy woodcuts and of many other outline woodcuts in books printed in the early 1490s. To the designer of these woodcuts, Hind gave the name the "Popular Designer," and suggested that he might have been a manuscript illuminator. As I have just indicated, I am convinced that Hind's "Popular Designer" was the miniaturist known as the Pico Master.

Hind also identified a second designer whom he called the "Classical Designer," rightly asserting that the famous *Hypnerotomachia poliphili* printed by Aldus Manutius in 1499 was this artist's greatest achievement in woodcut design.[8] An example of the handsome *Poliphilus* woodcuts represents Youths and Maidens Picking Flowers while surrounding a hero who is dressed in Roman military garb (fig. 1). As in the Pico Master's Livy woodcut, the figures are outlined and not shaded, but the figures are much fuller, the poses and costumes far more classical, justifying Hind's designation of the artist who designed them as the Classical Designer.

Here, however, the picture becomes considerably more complex. Even by the end of the 1490s, similar figures in Venetian woodcuts began to be modeled with parallel lines, leading to what Hind and others before him called the "shaded style," the third stage in this rapid development.[9] Exemplifying this innovation is a woodcut of the mythical hero Cephalus in Nicolò di Correggio's *La Psyche e La Aurora* of 1507.[10] Cephalus stands in virtually the same pose as the soldier in the *Poliphilus* woodcut, but his legs and tunic are modeled with closely cut parallel lines to heighten the sense of three-dimensionality. This shaded style requires greater technical skills by the cutter, but does not necessarily indicate that a different artist made the initial design.

The miniaturist Benedetto Bordon is linked by documents to the design of a major work in the shaded style, a series of twelve single-sheet woodcuts of a

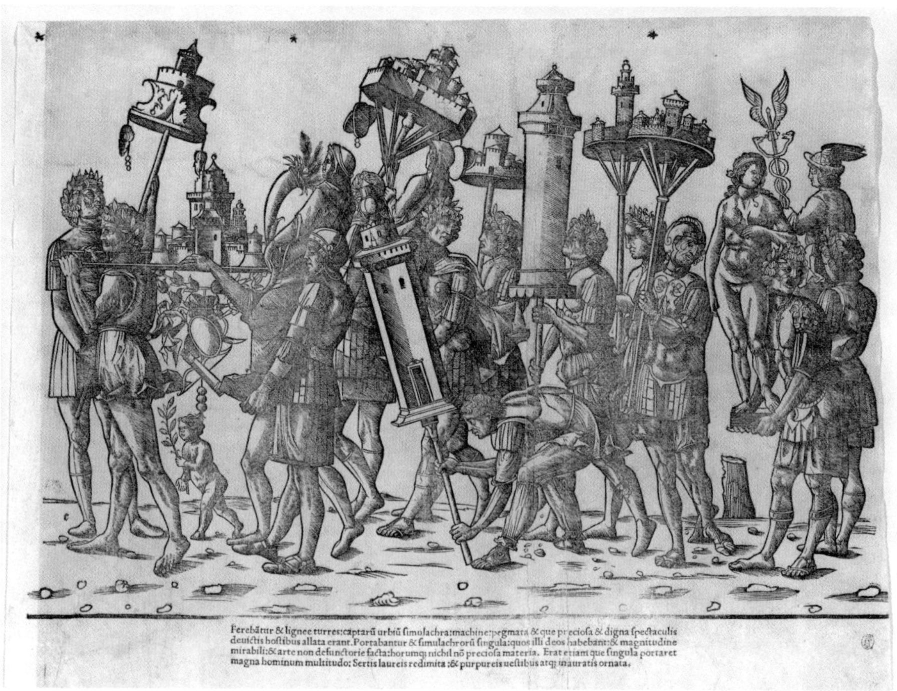

Fig. 2. Roman soldiers carrying models of conquered cities and statues of gods, from *Triumph of Caesar* series, woodcut designed by Benedetto Bordon and cut by Jacob of Strassburg, 1504 (The Metropolitan Museum of Art, Harris Brisbane Dick Fund, 1927. 27.54.121. Image © The Metropolitan Museum of Art).

Triumph of Caesar. In two closely argued articles, Jean Michel Massing showed that in 1504 Bordon designed the *Triumph* woodcuts, which were then cut by Jacob of Strassburg, a German craftsman who had begun to work in Venice around 1498.[11] Although the first state of this woodcut series bearing an inscription naming Jacob of Strasbourg was thought lost, it has now been recognized as extant in the Bibliothèque nationale de France.[12] The recognition that the *Triumph* woodcuts could certainly be ascribed to Benedetto Bordon was also an important breakthrough in understanding the illuminator's career. Earlier scholars had postulated that Bordon might have been the designer of the *Poliphilus* woodcuts, basing their arguments on comparisons with Bordon's miniatures. Now the *Poliphilus* woodcuts can also be compared with Bordon's *Triumphs* woodcuts.[13] The youthful hero of the *Poliphilus* seems cut out of the same

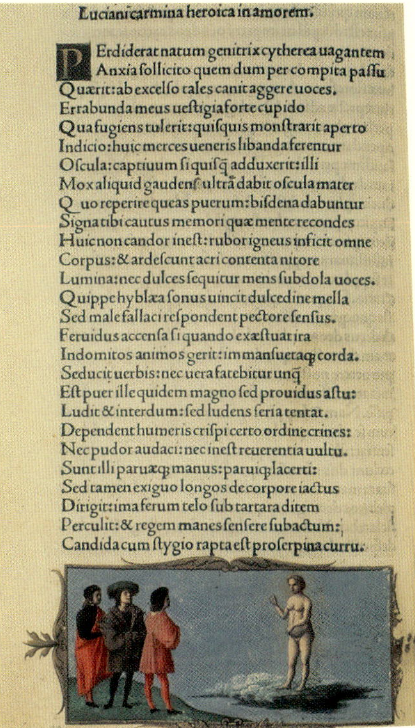

Luciani carmina heroica in amorem.

Perdiderat natum genitrix cytherea uagantem
Anxia sollicito quem dum per compita passu
Quærit: ab excelso tales canit aggere uoces.
Errabunda meus uestigia forte cupido
Qua fugiens tulerit: quisquis monstrarit aperto
Indicio: huic merces ueneris libanda ferentur
Oscula: captiuum si quisq̃ adduxerit: illi
Mox aliquid gaudens ultra dabit oscula mater
Quo reperire queas puerum: bis dena dabuntur
Signa tibi cautus memori quæ mente recondes
Huic non candor inest: rubor igneus inficit omne
Corpus: & ardescunt acri contenta nitore
Lumina: nec dulces sequitur mens subdola uoces.
Quippe hyblæa sonus uincit dulcedine mella
Sed male fallaci respondent pectore sensus.
Feruidus accensa si quando exæstuat ira
Indomitos animos gerit: immansuetaq; corda.
Seducit uerbis: nec uera fatebitur unq̃
Est puer ille quidem magno sed prouidus astu:
Ludit & interdum: sed ludens seria tentat.
Dependent humeris crispi certo ordine crines:
Nec pudor audaci: nec inest reuerentia uultu.
Sunt illi paruæq; manus: paruiq; lacerti:
Sed tamen exiguo longos de corpore iactus
Dirigit: ima ferum telo sub tartara ditem
Perculit: & regem manes sensere subactum:
Candida cum stygio rapta est proserpina curru.

Fig. 3. Venus Confronting Three Lovers, hand-painted miniature by Benedetto Bordon in Lucian, *Opera*, Venice, Simon Bevilaqua for Benedetto Bordon, 1494 (Vienna, Österreichische Nationalbibliothek, Inc. 4.G.27, fol. m8 verso [fol. 88 verso].).

Fig. 4. Alexander the Great, Scipio Africanus, and Hannibal before King Minos, hand-painted miniature by Benedetto Bordon in Lucian, *Opera*, Venice, Simon Bevilaqua for Benedetto Bordon, 1494 (Vienna, Österreichische Nationalbibliothek, Inc. 4.G.27, fol. h3 recto [fol. 55 recto]).

pattern as a frontally posed military figure in one of the *Triumph* woodcuts (fig. 2). In each case the figure stands with one foot firmly planted on the ground and the other drifting above it. The bending youth picking flowers is repeated in the soldier bent to raise a trophy; the crowds of figures are similarly spaced. These characteristics all bespeak a similar mode of composition, even though the heavy shading of the *Triumph* makes a contrasting first impression.

The visual connections between Bordon's woodcuts and his miniatures are further supported by observing female figures. In 1494, Benedetto Bordon painted miniatures in a copy of Lucian, now in Vienna, including an illustration for the story *Virtus dea.*[14] Standing in the foreground of a lovely landscape setting are Mercury, clad in Roman armor, and the goddess Virtue, nude. The slightly pudgy figure of Virtue resembles the statue held aloft by the struggling soldier in the *Triumph of Caesar* woodcut. Both nudes are posed in a marked contrapposto stance, and as in the stance of the soldiers, the relaxed leg seems to dangle somewhat uselessly above the ground or pedestal. Heavy shading articulates the high breasts and rounded belly; the turned head and straggly hair of the goddess provide further points of comparison. The same physical type is seen in a second Bordon miniature in the Vienna Lucian, Venus Confronting Three Lovers, although in this scene the goddess is posed in three-quarter view (fig. 3). These formal similarities reinforce the documentary evidence that ties the Vienna Lucian miniatures and the *Triumph* woodcuts to the same artist, Benedetto Bordon.

The 1494 Lucian, in and of itself, is important in linking Bordon to the two activities, since Bordon was himself its publisher and editor. The opening text page in all but one known copy is framed by a beautiful woodcut border consisting of delicate classical motifs in white on a black ground.[15] The unique copy now in Vienna, however, was printed on vellum without the woodcut border.[16] Instead, the opening page of the *True History* (*De veris narrationibus*) has a hand-illuminated border with golden bronze decorative motifs glowing against solid blue and green grounds. In the bottom margin is the coat of arms of the noble Mocenigo family of Venice. On the facing verso is a miniature illustrating Lucian and his companions meeting the farmer Scintharus, an event that transpired during their wanderings in the belly of a whale.

The layout of this small octavo Lucian is handsome, with wide margins, Roman type set in a single block, and several lines indented to reserve space for a painted initial. The fifteen narrative miniatures of the Vienna copy are positioned in the lower margins of folios on which a new text begins. These compositions of fanciful figures in simple settings form a useful backdrop for evaluating Bordon's probable design of woodcuts in the subsequent decades. Illustrating a section of the *Dialogues of the Dead* is a typical example showing Alexander the Great, Scipio, and Hannibal standing before an enthroned King Minos (fig. 4). The uncrowded spacing and quiet poses are characteristic of Bordon as are the brilliant colors and exquisite landscape with fluffy trees highlighted with gold. Alexander, dressed in red and yellow at the far left, leans slightly back on one leg as he extends the other in a pose typical of Bordon's standing figures. Since Bordon was the editor and publisher of the Lucian, virtually all scholars have accepted that he painted these miniatures in the Mocenigo presentation copy and that he designed the woodcut border found in the other copies of the edition.

A petition printed at the end of the 1494 Lucian provides fascinating material about Benedetto Bordon. In it, Bordon requests a privilege for the exclusive right to publish the book.[17] The request identifies Bordon as "*miniator*," that is, miniaturist or illuminator. He ingenuously asserts that the "works of Lucian... have never been printed before" (they had been), and that he "has worked hard in finding and emending these works." He further supports his request by stating "Given the great expense which he put forth in printing and editing these works, may your servant not abandon his work in vain, but rather may he be able to enjoy the fruit and honor from these works. . . ." Thus Bordon had claims to a sophisticated level of Latin learning, and he was anxious and willing to invest in a book that was to be printed at his expense. Bordon's enthusiasm for classical learning, his skill as a miniaturist, and his documented role as a designer of woodcuts leads to the question of what other images Bordon may have designed for classical texts.

Venetian Illustrated Classical Texts, 1490–1520

An exceptional number of classical texts illustrated with woodcuts were printed in Venice from 1490 to 1520.[18] A preliminary count of these editions reveals that books by thirty-eight Greek and Latin authors were published in editions that had at least one figural woodcut, and usually many more. Since many of the texts were printed more than once, the total is at least 204 editions.[19] By starting the count in 1490, the earliest Venetian texts by classical authors that have high numbers of woodcuts could be included. Around 1520 there is a very significant shift in the style of woodcuts produced, justifying the closing of the count at that date.

The sheer quantity of woodcuts suggested by these numbers is significant, but only a few of the original woodcuts are of high artistic quality. The first time a given text was illustrated, the printer or publisher needed to commission an artist to design woodcuts that were pertinent to that text, and these designs are most likely to be the strongest aesthetically. After the blocks were cut and printed for the first time, they were available for a later printing of the same text. Three further phenomena are also common. First, woodcuts originally designed for one text were frequently inserted into other, less appropriate texts. Secondly, woodcuts designed for one edition were often copied in variant woodcuts that were usually simpler, of lesser quality, and printed by a rival printer. Thirdly, a printer or publisher might commission an entirely new and different cycle of images for a popular text, presumably in hopes that the more up-to-date cycle would appeal to new buyers.

The period of the tabulated editions, 1490–1520, also falls within the chronological limits of Benedetto Bordon's career, since he was active from the late 1470s until his death in 1530. A complete discussion of these woodcut cycles is impossible within the confines of this paper, so a few examples must suffice to raise issues about Bordon and about the availability of classical imagery in this period.[20] An early yet typical edition is an Ovid, *Epistolae Heroides* printed in 1501 by Johannes Tacuinus, one of the most active printers of classical texts with woodcuts (fig. 5).[21] The size and layout differs from the 1494 Lucian and from the more familiar small Aldine octavo editions of the classics. It measures about 20 × 30 centimeters (or 8 × 12 inches), considerably larger than the 14 × 24 centimeters (5½ × 9½ inches) of the Lucian or the even smaller Aldines. The text proper is in Latin and is surrounded by a Latin commentary printed in a smaller roman font. Woodcut initials of various sizes initiate the text proper and sections of the commentary.

The shaded woodcut for the Letter from Ariadne to Theseus is fitted onto the page immediately above the text proper (see fig. 5). The woodcut is divided into three sections: at the left, Ariadne and her maid advise Theseus by a portal; in the center Theseus kills the Minotaur; at the right, the abandoned Ariadne is discovered by Bacchus as Theseus' ship departs in the background. It is interesting that the divine rescue by Bacchus is not mentioned in the text proper but instead is discussed in the commentary appearing close to the woodcut. Theseus is dressed as a Roman soldier, and his stance, swaying slightly back on one leg, echoes that of Bordon's Alexander in the 1494 Lucian in Vienna (see fig. 4). The division of the composition into three scenes permits the artist to distinguish several principal episodes, while their proximity on one rectangular block creates a certain level of unity. The areas of text and woodcut are quite well balanced, but the woodcut sits a bit uncomfortably above both text proper and commentary, and it projects slightly above the text into the upper margin as well.

A few years later another printer clearly believed he could improve on the 1501 publication. In 1506 Bartolomeus de Zanis issued an edition of the *Heroides* with a newly designed sequence of twenty-three woodcuts, in turn reissued with the new woodcuts again in 1507.[22] The overall layout of text proper, commentary, and woodcut initials is considerably more disciplined than in the 1501 edition. The woodcut is now almost square and more neatly fitted into the area above the text proper. But for the story of Ariadne and Theseus, the artist has apparently been ordered to include all three narrative episodes that appeared in the 1501 edition. Theseus confers with two women at the left, and at the right Ariadne is discovered by Bacchus. The slaying of the Minotaur has been relegated to the background and surrounded by the wall of the Labyrinth. The page has gained clarity, but the narrative has been compacted.

Both sequences show familiarity with Ovid's text. That these were not simply adaptations from the better-known stories of the *Metamorphoses* is demonstrated by the frequent inclusion of the heroine at a desk writing her letter. The image of a

ARIADNE THESEO

In decimam epistolam argumentum.

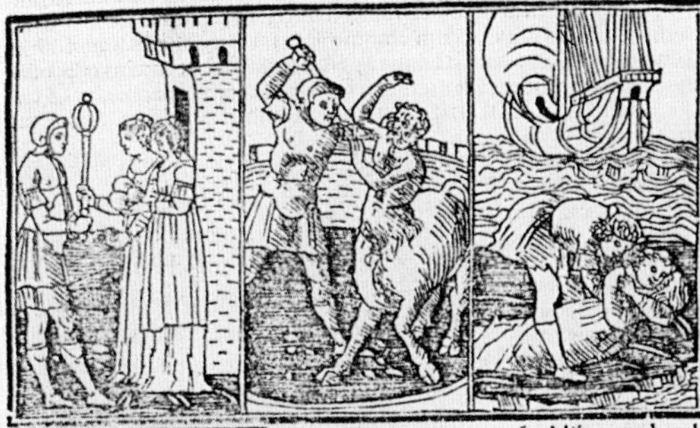

Itius inueni quã te genus oẽ ferarum. Glostenes & scriptores na xii duos fuisse Minoes scribũt: & totidem ariadnas priorem baccho in naxo insula nupsisse. Alteram uero a Theseo destitutam cum Corynam nutricem sequeretur in naxum nauigasse. Alii unicã ariadnã e creta raptã fuisse scribunt: & in naxo theseo relictam laqueo uitam finiuisse. Alii onaro bacchi sacerdoti desertam a nautis nupsisse: Ion chius ex Theseo Ariadnam peperisse œnopionem & Staphillum tradit. Peon Amatusius in sua historia affirmat Theseum cum Ariadne in Cyprum insulam esse ui tempestatis delatum illamque cum salo tabesceret incolis commendasse: post paulo cum rediret extinctam reperisse erexisseque illi duas statuas: argenteam alteram: alteram auream sacrificarique instituisse quarto calendas septembris. Ouidius uero cum Diodoro conuenit qui scribit Theseum cum Ariadna e creta soluentẽ in naxon esse delatum somnoque admonitum a Baccho: ut Ariadnam relinqueret dei timore perculsum puellam cum altissimo somno premeretur reliquisse: quam primum igitur expergefacta est: cum Theseum discessisse intelligeret hanc ad illum epistolam dedisse commentus est. Diodorus illud adiicit deductam a Baccho Ariadnam in montem qui Drios nuncupatur nunquam cõparuisse. ANTO.

ARIADNE THESEo.

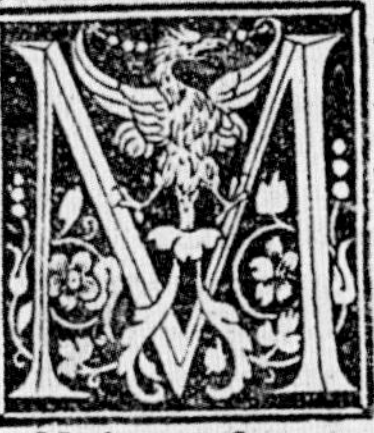

Itius inueni: quã te genus oẽ ferarum:
Credita nõ ulli: quã tibi peius eram.
Quæ legis: ex illo theseu tibi littore mitto:
Vnde tuam sine me uela tulere ratem.
In quo me somnusq; meus male pdidit: & tu
Per facinus somnis insidiate meis.
Tps erat uitrea quo primum terra pruina
Spargitur: & tectæ fronde queruntr aues.

MITIVS inueni quam te genus omne ferarum: in tota epistola perfidiæ est: & sæuitiæ expostulatio: quas a comparatione in principio statuit: Clementius inquit se mecum habuissent feræ & fidius custodissent: q̃ Theseus. CREdita: suæ fidei commissa translatio est a deposito. PEIVS: maiori perfidia. EX ILLo littore: patos a loco quem signat ne forte salutem alio translatam inuenisse Theseus existimaret: sum inquit in ea solitudine: in qua me reliquisti. PER facinus: purgat quod obiici potuisset: non mea culpa: sed tua pefidia relicta sum. TEMpus erat: inuidiam auget a tempore & circunstantiis: nam tempus locum & facti conditionem circunscribit. QVO primum terra pruina: matutinum crepusculum significat: quando terra leui rore immadescit.

Ariadne salutem dicit Theseo. VBER.

MITIVS inueni. Ne & chartas frustra impleam: & auditori sim fastidio non enarrabo iterum fabulam minotauri unde pendet argumentum huius epistolæ: quoniam satis dictum est in secunda epistola Phyllidis ad Demophoonta super eum locum. & Tauri mixtaq; forma uiri: & item in argumento epistolæ Phædræ ad Hippolitum: itaq; qui uelit plene uidere: illuc recurrat: quod autem ad hunc locum attinet: hoc est in summa: Cum ob leges a Minoe deuictis Atheniensibus impositas Theseus in Cretam nauigasset: Ariadne Minois filia eius specie ac decore capta consilium operamq; dedit Minotauri occidendi: & Labyrinthi egressum edocuit. Deinde cum Ariadne noctu clam recedens in insulam appulit aliquando Diam: nunc uero Naxon uocitatã: ubi dicitur reliquisse Ariadnem: & sine ea in patriam nauigasse. Quare fingit poeta eam derelictam scribere hanc epistolam ad Theseum: & eum increpare de duritia & immanitate animi & ingratitudine beneficiorum: quæ ei commemorat: & post commemoratas etiam infelicitates suas rogat eum: ut nauem flectat: & redeat ad eam recipiendam. MITIus: id est minus crudele: nam nulla fera mitis est. CREdita: id est commissa. tradita. VLLi: alicui siue homini siue feræ. VNDe: id est ex quo scilicet littore. TVLere: pro abstulere. SOMnus: id est sopor. ET tu: scilicet prodidisti. TEMpus erat: dicit fuisse autumnale tempus. VITrea: splendida ut uitrum. SPARgitur: impletur. PRVinis: Iuuenalis. Iam læti ferro cedente. PRVinis: autumno.

i ii

Fig. 5. Letter from Ariadne to Theseus, woodcut in Ovid, Epistolae Heroides, Venice, Johannes Tacuinus, 10 July 1501, fol. i2 recto (Cambridge, MA, Harvard University, Houghton Library, Typ 525.01.663).

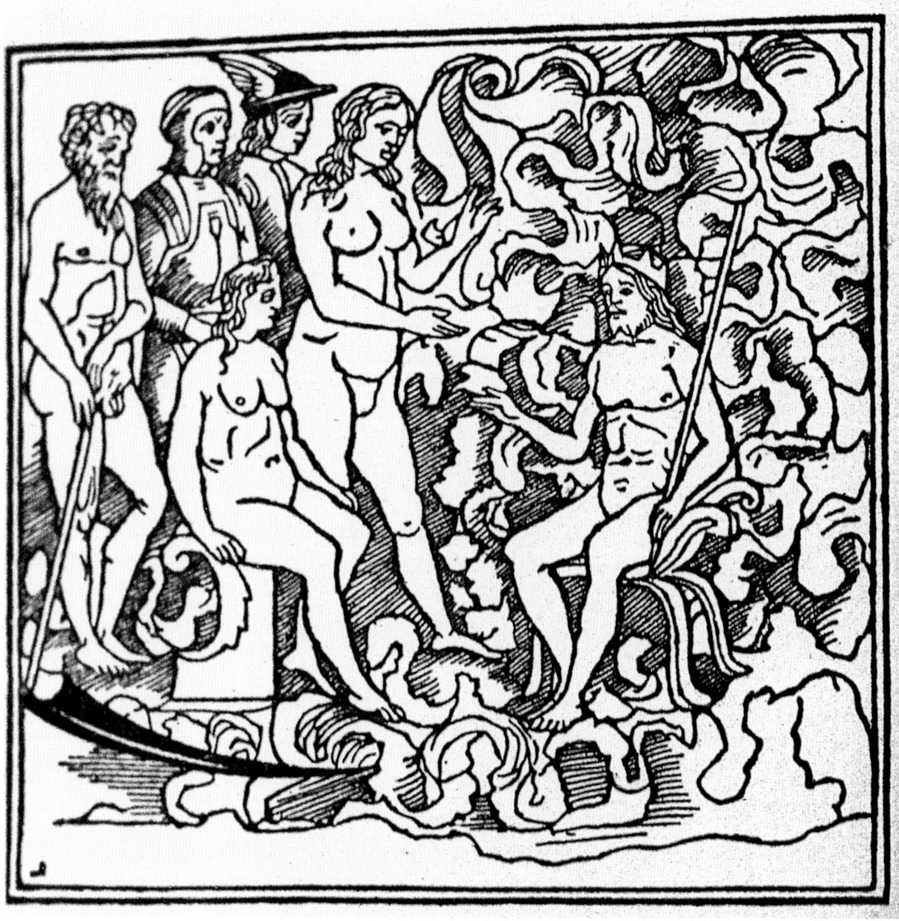

Fig. 6. Council of the Gods, woodcut in Virgil, *Opera*, Venice, Philippus Pintius, 15 September 1505, fol. M1 recto (fol. 289 recto), *Aeneid*, Book 10, woodcut design attributed to Benedetto Bordon (from Victor Masséna, Prince d'Essling, *Les livres à figures vénetiens de la fin du XV siècle et du commencement du XVI siècle*, Florence, 1907–1914, Part 1, Vol. 1, p. 63, reproducing the woodcut from Virgil, Opera, Venice, Bartolomaeus de Zanis, 3 August 1508, fol. 314 verso).

woman writing appropriately belongs to the *Epistolae* and is not borrowed from the *Metamorphoses.*[23]

The case of the Virgil illustration is particularly interesting, and the woodcuts for the first illustrated edition also contain many echoes of works by Benedetto Bordon. Thanks to the research of Craig Kallendorf, a Virgil printed in 1505 is now thought to be the earliest edition illustrated with woodcuts, containing a total of twenty newly composed figurative images.[24] These include two author portrait woodcuts on the title page, one pastoral scene at the opening of the *Bucolics,* four agricultural images for the *Georgics,* twelve narrative episodes for Virgil's *Aeneid,* and finally another narrative scene at the beginning of Maphaeus Vegius' Book XIII. The format of the 1505 Virgil is very close to that of the *Heroides* 1506 edition, although it was printed by Philippus Pintius rather than the prolific Johannes Tacuinus. On the page opening the *Bucolics* are represented Tityrus and Meliboeus in a landscape setting.[25] Meliboeus leans on his shepherd's staff, standing in a frontal pose not unlike a soldier in Bordon's *Triumph of Caesar* of 1504 (see fig. 2) or Cephalus in the *Cephalus and Aurora* woodcut of 1507.[26] Tityrus is seated at the base of a tree, playing a bagpipe; beside him lies a faithful dog. Around this same date Bordon provided a monochrome miniature in a manuscript of Virgil in which Meliboeus also stands with crossed legs leaning on a staff, and Tityrus is seated beneath a tree playing pan pipes.[27] The grove of trees and the walled town in the background of the woodcut are also compositional components found in Bordon's miniatures for the 1494 Lucian in Vienna. The representation of two shepherds to initiate the *Bucolics,* however, is typical of Virgil illustration as far back as the *Roman Virgil* of the late fifth century.[28]

When the artist turns to Dido's Banquet he is more innovative. Dido, wearing a Phrygian hat because she was of Phoenician heritage, sits on a table in pseudo-oriental fashion. She faces Aeneas, who wears a Turkish turban since he came from Troy, in the sixteenth century controlled by the Turks. The dog in the foreground echoes the dog in the Scinthaurus miniature of the Vienna Lucian, mentioned above, and similarly rendered pets are found in more than one of Bordon's religious miniatures.[29] Attendants further enrich the scene; the standing veiled woman at the left adheres closely to the model set by Anna in the woodcut of the Meeting of Anna and Joachim composed by Bordon for *Graduale romanum,* printed by LucAntonio Giunta in 1499–1501.[30]

Perhaps more expected in a culture enthused about classical antiquity is the Council of the Gods, illustrating Book 10 of the *Aeneid* (fig. 6). Jupiter, nude and enveloped by clouds, sits opposite Juno. Behind Juno are ranged Venus, Mercury, Mars, and Saturn, all with suitable attributes. There are strong resemblances between the nudes of the Council of the Gods and Bordon's female figures in the 1494 Lucian in Vienna. In the miniature of Venus Confronting Three Lovers, Bordon depicts his usual softly modeled nude standing on a cloud (see fig. 3). Her pose, with the right hand lifted in a gesture of admonition and the left arm reaching across the goddess' belly, is virtually identical in the two images. In the Lucian miniature, however, the goddess confronts three young men gaudily dressed in the latest Venetian fashions.

Dido's Banquet and the Council of the Gods are also examples of woodcuts that a printer was happy to reemploy in a new context. In a Horace printed by Donino

Pintius a few months after the 1505 Virgil, the woodcut of Dido's Banquet illustrates Book IV, Ode 8, *Ad Censorinum;* while the Council of the Gods somewhat more understandably illustrates Book IV, Ode 1, *Ad venerem.*[31] Why commission a new design for Horace, if your relative has a handsome woodblock or two that would do almost as well?

Illustrations of Ovid and Virgil, authors with long traditions of miniatures in manuscripts, might well be expected in Venetian woodcuts of the early sixteenth century. But more unexpected is a cycle of almost forty newly composed woodcuts for an edition of Cicero's *De Officiis,* printed by the energetic Johannes Tacuinus in 1506 [1507], and reprinted four more times before 1520.[32] In each case the edition also included Cicero's *De Amicitia* and *De Senectute.* The striking frontispiece of *De Senectute* in the 1506 [1507] edition (fig. 7) is better designed than that of the 1501 Ovid *Heroides.*[33] The printer has chosen a blackground woodcut border that balances the dark block of text, blackground initial, and the large shaded woodcut of the enthroned elder and the two youthful soldiers.

Many of the forty smaller woodcuts are equally handsome, with dignified figures in quiet poses and set against spreading landscapes. For example, two Roman soldiers clasp hands to illustrate the Just Treatment of an Enemy.[34] The soldiers here, as in the *De Senectute* frontispiece, lean back on one foot in poses that are highly reminiscent of Alexander in Bordon's 1494 Lucian miniature of Alexander, Scipio, and Hannibal before King Minos described above (see fig. 4). Their costumes also correspond with those of the Roman soldiers in Bordon's *Triumph of Caesar* (see fig. 2).[35]

Three other woodcuts suggest the flexibility and inflexibility of the imagery. They appear on facing folios in a section of the text in which Cicero discusses promises that should not be kept (fols. 184 verso and 185 recto). Firstly, Cicero posits that if Phaeton's father, Sol, had not kept his promise to grant any wish of his son, the son would not have had to be destroyed.[36] The woodcut for this section represents the Ride of Phaeton. In the upper part of the scene, Phaeton triumphantly drives the chariot of the sun, but below and to the right, flames leap up signaling his lack of control and eventual doom. The image is indeed appropriate for Cicero's text, but given its mythological subject, it could easily be reused to illustrate a mythological text in addition to this philosophical one.

On the facing page, Cicero discusses the dilemma faced when "a person leaves his sword with you when he is in his right mind, and demands it back in a fit of insanity."[37] In the illustrative woodcut, the action takes place in two phases: in the active phase at the right, the youth holds the sword upright, and in a more complex moment on the left, the sword is held downwards while the young man looks hesitantly over his shoulder. The designer must have understood the text or have had it explained to him

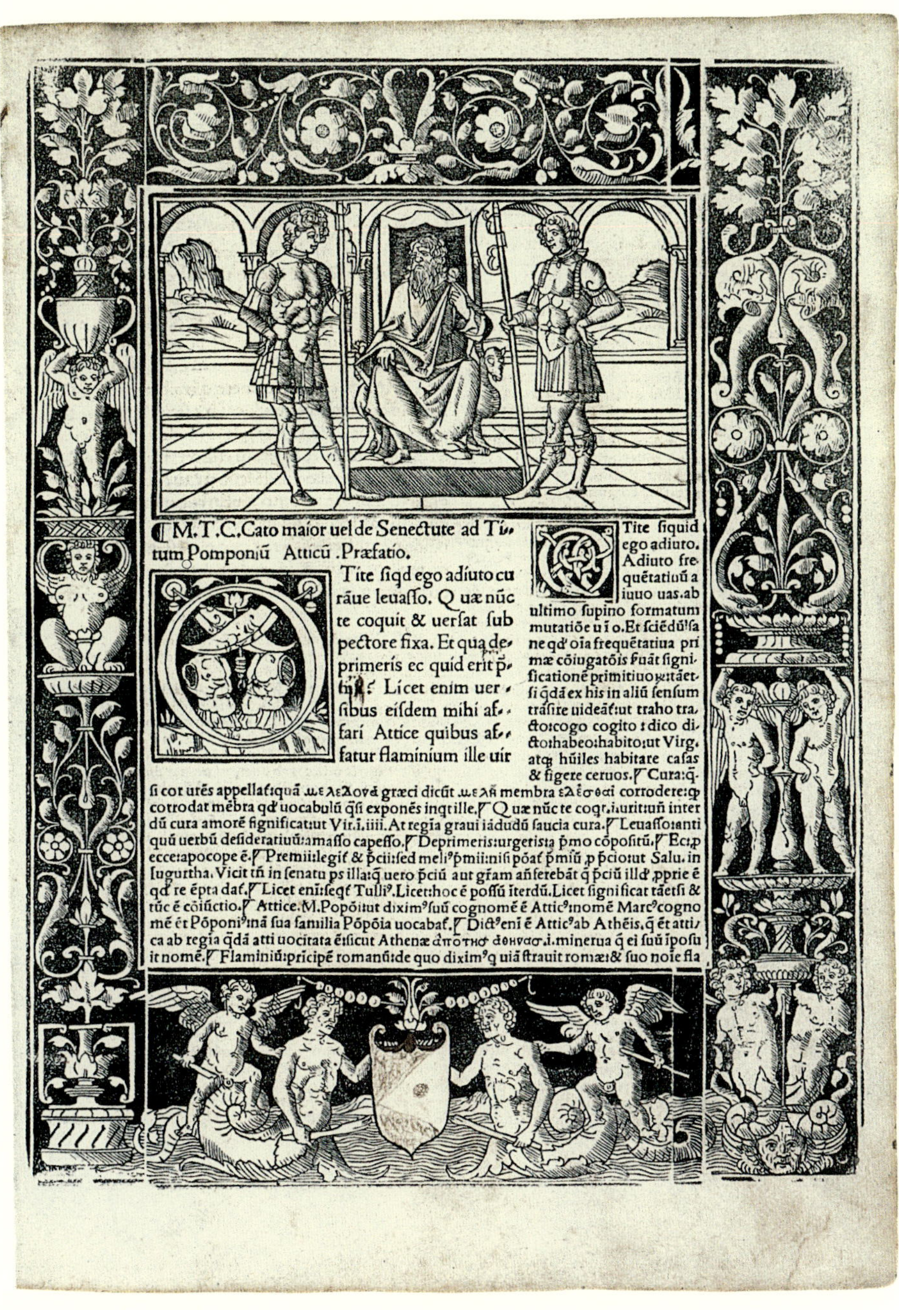

M.T.C. Cato maior uel de Senectute ad Titum Pomponiũ Atticũ. Præfatio.

Tite ſiqd ego adiuto cu rãue leuaſſo. Quæ nũc te coquit & uerſat ſub pectore fixa. Et quã depreſſeris ec quid erit p̃tii? Licet enim uerſibus eiſdem mihi affari Attice quibus affatur flaminium ille uir

Tite ſiquid ego adiuto. Adiuto frequẽtatiuũ a iuuo uas. ab ultimo ſupino formatum mutatiõe u i o. Et ſciẽdũ'ſa ne qd' oĩa frequẽtatiua primæ cõiugatõis ſuãt ſignificationẽ primitiuo: etſi qdã ex his in aliũ ſenſum trãſire uideãt: ut traho tracto: cogo cogito: dico dicto: habeo: habito: ut Virg. atq; hũiles habitare caſas & figere ceruos. Cura: q̃ſi cor urẽs appellat: quã μελεδονα græci dicũt μελη membra ἐδεσθαι corrodere: q̃ corrodat mẽbra qd' uocabulũ q̃ſi exponẽs inqt ille. Quæ nũc te coqt. i. urit: uñ interdũ cura amorẽ ſignificat: ut Vir. i. iiii. At regia graui iãdudũ ſaucia cura. Leuaſſo: anti quũ uerbũ deſideratiuũ: amaſſo capeſſo. Deprimeris: urgeris: ta p̃mo cõpoſitũ. Ec: p ecce: apocope ẽ. Premii: legit & p̃cii: ſed meli⁹ p̃mii: niſi põat p̃miũ p p̃cio: ut Salu. in Iugurtha. Vicit tñ in ſenatu ps illa: q̃ uero p̃ciũ aut grãm añferebãt q̃ p̃ciũ illd' p̃prie ẽ qd' re ẽpta dat. Licet eni: ſeqt Tulli⁹. Licet: hoc ẽ poſſũ iterdũ. Licet ſignificat tãetſi & tũc ẽ cõiũctio. Attice. M. Põpõi: ut dixim⁹ ſuũ cognomẽ ẽ Attic⁹: nomẽ Marc⁹ cognomẽ ẽt Põponi⁹ nã ſua familia Põpõia uocabat. Dict⁹ eni ẽ Attic⁹ ab Athẽis. q̃ ẽt attica ab regia q̃dã atti uocitata ẽ: ſicut Athenæ [illegible] [illegible]. i. minerua q̃ ei ſuũ iPoſuit nomẽ. Flaminiũ: pricipẽ romanũ: de quo dixim⁹ q uiã ſtrauit romæ: & ſuo noie fla

Fig. 7. Young Roman Soldiers and an Enthroned Elder, and a blackground border with classical motifs, woodcut frontispiece for *De Senectute in Cicero, De Officiis, Etc*, Venice, Johannes Tacuinus, 20 February 1506 [1507], fol. DD4 recto (fol. 208 recto), woodcut design attributed to Benedetto Bordon (Cambridge, MA, Harvard University, Houghton Library, Lc 38.738*).

in detail, because the woodcut is very specifically tied to it. It is also harder to imagine the reuse of the image, in contrast to the Phaeton woodcut. The third woodcut on the opening is much more generic: a woman struggles with a lion, personifying the virtue of Fortitude. Cicero is indeed discussing the need for fortitude, but one could easily imagine other texts into which this woodcut could be inserted.

Cicero's *De Officiis* would have had particular appeal to the Venetian patriciate, who were greatly concerned with the correct behavior of public officials both in Venice and on the *terra firma*.[38] The woodcuts for this edition visualize Cicero's abstract ideas in a rich variety of images, insuring its popularity and many subsequent printings.

Evidence of Model Drawings: Images of Attack and Transformation

FURTHER LINKS between Venetian woodcuts in classical texts and Benedetto Bordon's miniatures can be seen in a series of images of attack. Medieval and Renaissance miniaturists retained model drawings in their workshops that could be adapted to meet various compositional demands.[39] One composition that must have depended on such a model can be traced through several of the classical texts under consideration. In an amusing miniature several times analyzed by Helena Szépe, Benedetto Bordon depicted the angry author Juvenal literally "throwing the book" at a group of retreating Vices.[40] This painted composition, found in a copy of Aldus Manutius' Juvenal printed in 1501, is repeated in a witty woodcut revision in a second Juvenal printed in 1503.[41] In the woodcut, the book is violently thrown by a satyr, rather than the author, but the striding legs and raised right hand and arm strike the same pose. The probability that Bordon had created a drawing of this vigorous group even earlier than 1501 is suggested by a woodcut in the *Hypnerotomachia poliphili* of 1499 showing Polia and Poliphilus being chased out of the Temple of Diana.[42] The attackers are female and the weapons are clubs, but the striding poses replicate those of Juvenal and of the satyr.

In the Cicero, *De Officiis* of 1506 [1507], the constellation emerges again, this time to illustrate Two Kinds of Injustice.[43] Four figures appear in the foreground of a landscape which features distant trees and a rocky mountain. Rushing in from the left is a man wearing a short tunic and wielding a sword above his head. An older woman and a girl retreat in the center as the old woman raises her arm in a defensive gesture similar to that of a Vice in the Bordon Juvenal miniature. To the far right a short youth stands passively observing the attack. The artist has captured Cicero's designation of the unjust primarily as "those who inflict wrong," and secondarily as "those who do not shield from wrong those on whom it is inflicted."[44]

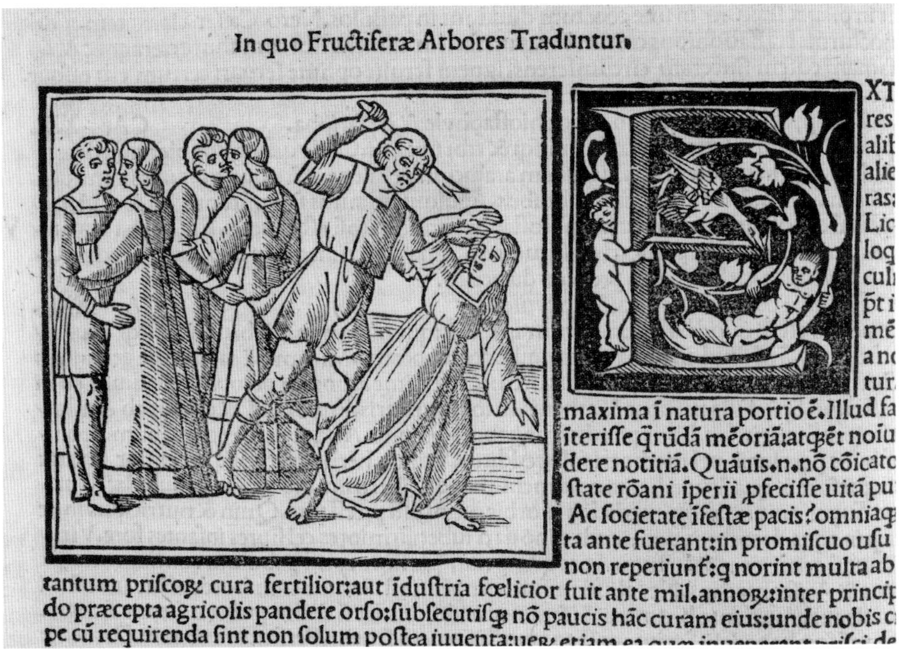

Fig. 8. Lovers and an Angry Man Attacking Women, woodcut in Pliny, *Historia naturalis*, Venice, Melchior Sessa, 20 August 1513, fol. K8 verso, Book 14, woodcut design attributed to Benedetto Bordon (London, British Library, 442.h.2 [1] © The British Library, All Rights Reserved).

Still later, in 1513, an inventive cycle of thirty-seven woodcuts was created for an edition of Pliny's *Historia naturalis* printed by Melchior Sessa.[45] Toward the end of Book 14 on the Vintage, Pliny describes the distressing effects of excessive drinking.[46] In the woodcut of 1513, our lunging attacker appears again, to illustrate Pliny's comment that many a person has lost his life as a result of insults uttered when inebriated (fig. 8). Two embracing couples reflect the licentious behavior equally inspired by wine. The enraged attacker wearing a short tunic brandishes a thick stick and looms over a girl who leans away and tries to protect herself with an upraised arm. The somewhat clumsy application of the model drawing is revealed by the way in which the striker's leg and foot hover above the floor rather than being placed firmly on it. Three years later in a Plutarch of 1516, also printed by Sessa, the attack is transferred to the Assassination of Julius Caesar, with Caesar lost in the folds of his toga as he is beset by his enemies.[47] These frequent repetitions indicate that the master drawing in Bordon's workshop was available to be applied whenever a violent subject needed to be represented.

The final illustrated classical text to be mentioned allows us to conclude on a less vehement note. A cycle of woodcuts in Bordon's style was designed for an Italian

tutti li diti preducano il numero in ungia ſono congion-
ti, ſora de la ſpina uiene una gran coda, la faccia fora di
miſura e le nara aperte & i labri pendenti, ma ſopra il
tutto le orechie grande faccio e peloſo, Ne alchuna coſa
piaceuole in queſta tranſmutatione me ueniaſe non la na
tura a Fotide baſtante e ſoperchia che conſiderandomi
tutto mi uegio aſino fatto, & non uccello & gia priua
to di geſto & uoce humana.

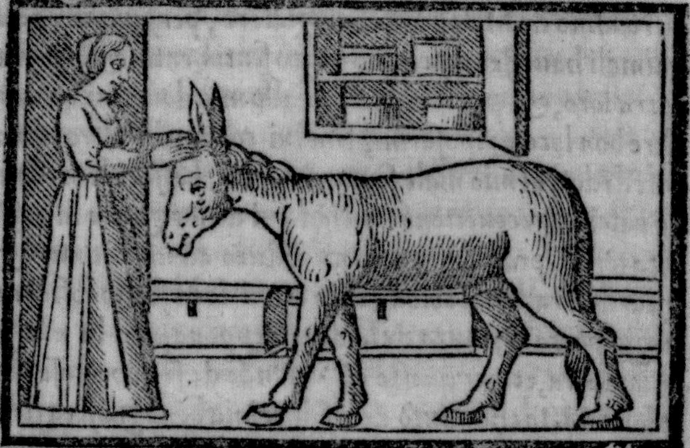

QVello che ſolo potea battendo il labro di ſotto
con li humidi ochi guardaua Fotide a trauer
ſo, lei come prima tal me uide dandoſe le ma
ne nel uiſo, Io ſon morta miſera me cridaua, la freza e la
paura mha ingannata & la ſimilitudine di buſeli, ma
nel male bene e aduenuto che la reformatione di queſto
molto e piu legiera, Imperho che ſolamente mordendo le
roſe uſcirai di queſto aſino e tornarai pure il mio Lucio,
coſi uoleſſe dio che come io ſolea haueſſe apparechiato la
corona de roſe, Ma comportati queſta notte che al pri

D

Fig. 9. Photis and Lucius Transformed into an Ass, woodcut in Apuleius, *Asinus Aureus* (in Italian). Venice, Niccolò Zoppino and Vincenzo di Paolo, 10 September 1518, fol. D1 recto, woodcut design attributed to Benedetto Bordon (Cambridge, MA, Department of Printing and Graphic Arts, Houghton Library, Harvard College Library, Typ 525.18.225).

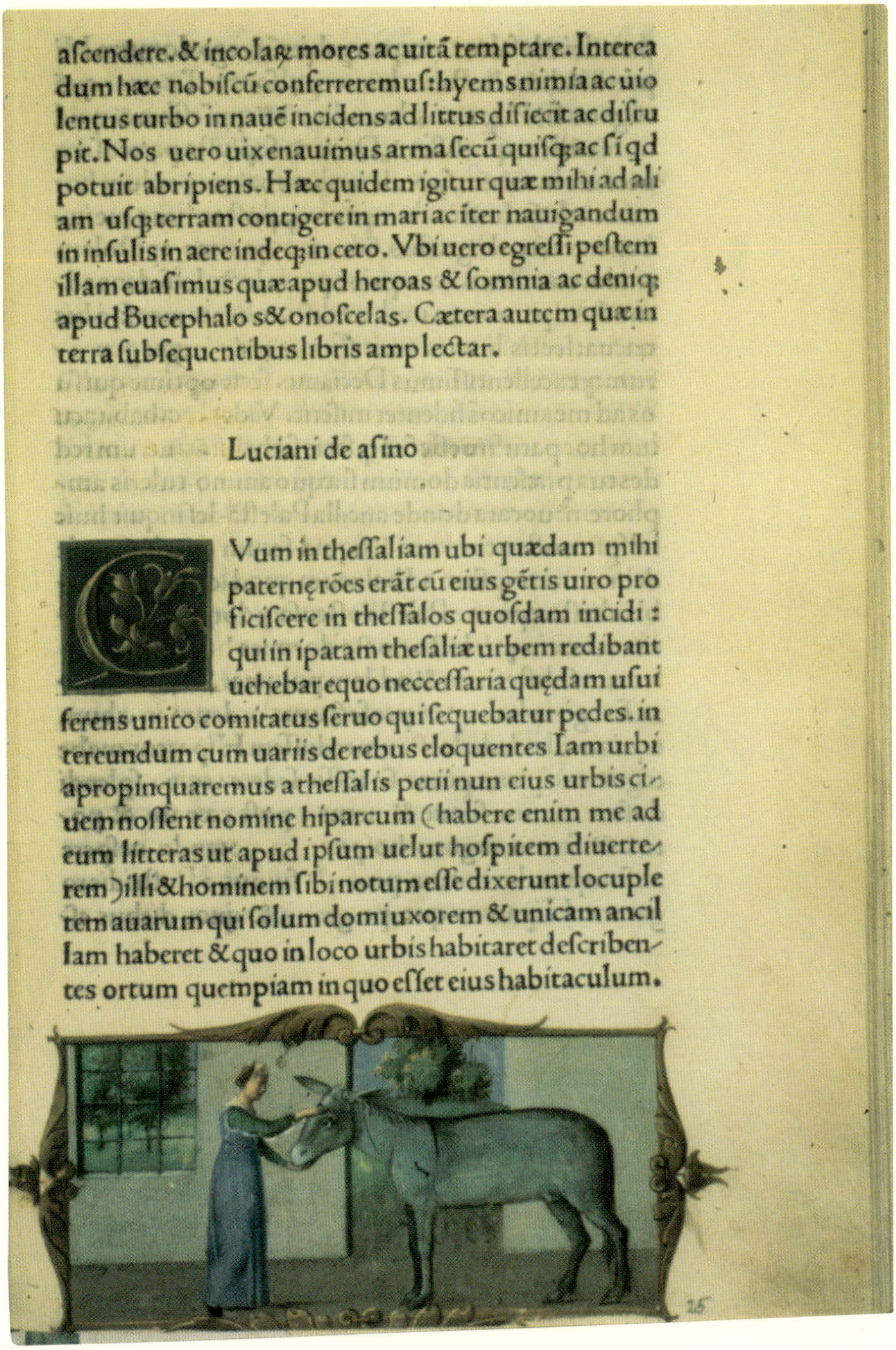

ascendere. & incolarum mores ac uitã temptare. Interea
dum hæc nobiscũ conferreremus: hyems nimia ac uio
lentus turbo in nauẽ incidens ad littus disiecit ac disru
pit. Nos uero uix enauimus arma secũ quisq; ac si qd
potuit abripiens. Hæc quidem igitur quæ mihi ad ali
am usq; terram contigere in mari ac iter nauigandum
in insulis in aere indeq; in ceto. Vbi uero egressi pestem
illam euasimus quæ apud heroas & somnia ac deniq;
apud Bucephalos & onoscelas. Cætera autem quæ in
terra subsequentibus libris amplectar.

Luciani de asino

CVum in thessaliam ubi quædam mihi
paternę rões erãt cũ eius gẽtis uiro pro
ficiscere in thessalos quosdam incidi:
qui in ipatam thesaliæ urbem redibant
uehebar equo neccessaria quędam usui
ferens unico comitatus seruo qui sequebatur pedes. in
tereundum cum uariis de rebus eloquentes Iam urbi
apropinquaremus a thessalis petii nun eius urbis ci-
uem nossent nomine hiparcum (habere enim me ad
eum litteras ut apud ipsum uelut hospitem diuerte-
rem) illi & hominem sibi notum esse dixerunt locuple
tem auarum qui solum domi uxorem & unicam ancil
lam haberet & quo in loco urbis habitaret describen-
tes ortum quempiam in quo esset eius habitaculum.

Fig. 10. Palestra and Lucius transformed into an Ass, hand-painted miniature by Benedetto Bordon in Lucian, *Opera*, Venice, Simon Bevilaqua for Benedetto Bordon, 1494 (Vienna, Österreichische Nationalbibliothek, Inc. 4.G.27, fol. d5 recto [fol. 25 recto]).

translation of Apuleius, *Asinus Aureus* (the *Golden Ass*), printed in 1518 by Niccolò Zoppino and Vincenzo di Paolo.[48] The *Golden Ass* is a text derived ultimately from Lucian's *Lucius, or the Ass*, one of the tales that Bordon claimed to have edited some twenty-four years earlier.[49] The 1518 Apuleius edition revives the Aldine small octavo book in its format, italic font, and lack of commentary. But the popularity of illustrated texts has had its impact, and there are thirty-two finely executed woodcuts in the edition, each carefully fitted within the width of the printed block of text (fig. 9). They are newly designed with charming images that closely correspond to the fanciful tales. The compositions and the cutting are refined, unlike the woodcuts in the 1510 edition, which were aptly described by Essling as mediocre.[50]

In size, arrangement of the figures, and settings, the Apuleius woodcuts vividly recall Benedetto Bordon's miniatures in the 1494 Lucian in Vienna. In the miniature illustrating *Lucius, or the Ass*, Bordon depicts Lucius' mistress, Palestra, patting his head after Lucius has been transformed into an ass. Dressed in a simple long blue robe, Palestra stands in profile reaching both arms out toward the patient ass. Behind them grey walls of a building are interrupted by openings through which appear verdant trees. The poses and simple setting find close parallels in the Apuleius woodcut. The mistress, in this case named Photis, likewise faces Lucius in his metamorphized state (figs. 9–10). The pair inhabits a simple interior with a back wall parallel to the picture plane. Above the ass a cupboard opens to reveal the boxes of unguent containers, the source of Lucius' erroneous transformation. I suggest that the close parallel between the miniature and the woodcut of the same subject testifies to their similar origin in Benedetto Bordon's workshop, where a model drawing served as the basis for both compositions.

Conclusion

THE PRECEDING EXAMPLES of illustrated Venetian books printed between 1490 and 1520 support the notion that a vast reservoir of "classical" imagery was available in the artistically crucial decades of the early Cinquecento. I would also argue that Benedetto Bordon designed woodcuts for a significant number of the classical editions printed in these years. The outline of his known commissions suggests that there was ample time for such design work. Relatively few manuscript projects can be attributed to Bordon in the period 1500–20. His work illuminating six choirbooks for San Nicolò dei Frari was probably completed around 1500–5, and his illuminated Aldines and Books of Hours were primarily executed shortly after 1500.[51] A major project designing woodcuts for liturgical books was also concentrated in the period 1499–1503.[52] From 1492 to 1528,

Bordon and his workshop illuminated some thirty-four *ducali,* but these official state documents normally contained only one or at most two miniatures.[53] Not until 1523 did he receive the manuscript commission which was to be the crowning event of his long career, the great *Evangeliarium* for Santa Giustina in Padua, containing seventy-four narrative miniatures and many exquisite borders.[54]

Of the relatively few renowned miniaturists active in Venice in this period, Bordon was the one with the greatest experience dealing with printers. As was discussed above, Bordon is documented working with a professional cutter, Jacob of Strassburg, and the printers for whom he did designs would have employed a variety of cutters as well. Commissions for woodcut designs would have been welcome to this prolific artist, especially those that drew upon his enthusiasm for the classics. As his edition of Lucian and his woodcut *Triumph of Caesar* testify, he was exceptionally learned for a Renaissance "craftsman."[55] Bordon's profile thus fits Hind's definition of the "Classical Designer" whose presence loomed over woodcut production in this period, regardless of who he was.

NOTES

I wish to express my gratitude to Daniel De Simone for having invited me to participate in *The Heavenly Craft* symposium at which this paper was presented, and for all the help and encouragement he offered in the preparation of it for publication.

Abbreviated Sources

Essling = Victor Masséna, Prince d'Essling, *Les livres à figures Vénetiens de la fin du XVe siècle et du commencement du XVIe,* 6 vols., Paris and Florence, 1907–14.

H, HC, R = L. R. T. Hain, *Repertorium Bibliographicum,* 2 vols. in 4 (Stuttgart, 1826–38); W. A. Copinger, *Supplement* (London, 1895–1902); D. Reichling, *Appendices* (1905–14)

Sander = Max Sander, *Le livre à figures italien depuis 1467 jusqu'en 1530,* 6 vols. (Milan, 1942).

1. For an informative survey of Venetian painting see Peter Humfrey, *Venetian Renaissance Painting* (New Haven, CT: Yale University Press, 1995).

2. Lilian Armstrong, "Venetian and Florentine Renaissance Woodcuts for Bibles, Liturgical Books, and Devotional Books," in *A Heavenly Craft: The Woodcut in Early Printed Books,* exh. cat., ed. Daniel De Simone (Washington, DC: Library of Congress, 2004), 25–45.

On Benedetto Bordon see Myriam Billanovich, "Benedetto Bordon e Giulio Cesare Scaligero," *Italia medioevale e umanistica* 11 (1968): 187–256; Giordana Mariani Canova, *La miniatura veneta del Rinascimento* (Venice: Alfieri, 1969), 69–74, 122–30, 156–57; Ulrike Bauer-Eberhardt, "Cima, Benedetto Bordon e il Maestro delle sette virtù: nuove attribuzioni e coincidenze," *Venezia cinquecento* 4, no. 7 (1994): 103–25; Helena K. Szépe, "The Book as Companion, The Author as Friend: Aldine Octavos Illuminated by Benedetto Bordon," *Word and Image* 11 (1995): 77–99; and Lilian Armstrong, "Benedetto Bordon, Aldus Manutius, LucAntonio Giunta: Old Links and New," in *Aldus Manutius and Renaissance Culture,* ed. David Zeidberg, Villa I Tatti, The Harvard University Center for Italian Renaissance Studies, vol. 15 (Florence: Leo S. Olschki, 1998), 161–183, all with further bibliography.

3. *Antiphonarium* (detached leaves), Biblioteca Apostolica Vaticana, MS Ross. 1195, fol. 28r (Armstrong, "Venetian and Florentine Woodcuts," fig. 14); *Missale romanum,* Venice, LucAntonio Giunta, 20 November 1501, fol. 158v, item 738 in *The Lessing J. Rosenwald Collection, 1943 to 1975* (Washington, DC: Library of Congress, 1977) and item 39 *A Heavenly Craft* (cited in note 2); *Breviarium romanum,* Venice, LucAntonio Giunta, 26 March 1507, item 758 in LC/Rosenwald and item 44 in *A Heavenly Craft.*

4. H. 13105. Location unknown. L. Armstrong, "The Pico Master: A Venetian Miniaturist of the Late Quattrocento," in Armstrong, *Studies of Renaissance Miniaturists* (London: Pindar Press, 2003), 233–338, esp. 250–51, 321 [cat. no. 40], and Pl. 18; illustrated in color in London, Christie's, *The Library of William Foyle, Part II: Early Continental Books,* 11 July 2000, Lot 254.

5. Livius, *Historiae Romanae decades* (in Italian), Venice, Johannes Rubeus Vercellensis for LucAntonio Giunta, 1493 (HC 10149; E. 33; Sander, no. 3397; Lilian Armstrong, "The Illustrated Livy of 1493," in *Vision of a Collector: The Lessing J. Rosenwald Collection in the Library of Congress* (Washington, DC: Library of Congress, 1991), fig. 36.

6. London, Sotheby's, *Catalogue of the Magnificent Library . . . C. W. Dyson Perrins, Part I, Books Printed in Italy,* June 17–18, 1946, Lot 221; and see above note 4; and Armstrong, "The Illustrated Livy," pp. 168–171, fig. 36.

7. New York and London, 1935 (reprint, 2 vols. New York, 1963), pp. 464–506.

8. [Francesco Colonna], *Hypnerotomachia Poliphili* Venice, Aldus Manutius, 1499, fol. b6 recto (HC 5501; E. 1198; Sander 2056). The literature on the text and illustrations of the *Hypnerotomachia Poliphili* is vast. See G. Pozzi and L. Ciapponi, *Hypnerotomachia Poliphili. Edizione critica e commento* (Padua, 1980, reprint of 1964 ed. with new critical review of literature); Helena K. Szépe, *The Poliphilo and Other Aldines Reconsidered in the Context of the Production of Decorated Books in Venice* (unpublished Ph.D. dissertation, Cornell University, Ithaca, NY, 1991); Bauer-Eberhardt; *Verso il Polifilo, 1499–1999,* San Donà di Piave, 31 October–8 November 1998, exhibition catalogue and essays, ed. Dino Casagrande and Alessandro Scarsella (*Miscellaneo Marciana,* 13

[1998]); Helena K. Szépe, "Artistic Identity in the *Poliphilo*," *Papers of the Bibliographical Society of Canada* 35 (1997): 39–73. Two recent translations are: *Hypnerotomachia Poliphili*, Italian trans. [and commentary] by Marco Ariani and Mino Gabriele, 2 vols. (Milan, 1999); and *Hypnerotomachia Poliphili: The Strife of Love in a Dream*, English trans. by Joscelyn Godwin (London: Thames and Hudson, 1999).

9. The "shaded style" is already articulated by Essling, *Les livres à figures Vénetiens*, Partie III, pp. 93ff.

10. Nicolò da Correggio, *La Psyche e La Aurora*. Venice, Manfredo da Monteferrato, 10 June 1507, fol. G3 verso (BL G.10645; E. 1566; Sander, 2212; illus. in Essling, II, I, p. 150).

11. Jean Michel Massing, "Jacobus Argentoratensis: Étude Préliminaire," *Arte veneta* 31 (1977): 42–52; and Jean Michel Massing, "The Triumph of Caesar by Benedetto Bordone and Jacobus Argentoratensis: Its Iconography and Influence," *Print Quarterly* 7 (1990): 2–21. A complete set of the *Triumph* woodcuts is in Berlin, Staatliche Museen Preussischer Kulturbesitz, Kupferstichkabinett, *Triumph of Caesar* (Accession no. 344-38).

12. Paris, Bibliothèque nationale de France, Cabinet des Estampes, Rés. *Ea 19, in fol. The author identified these prints in July 2006 and discusses them in detail in Lilian Armstrong, "The Triumph of Caesar Woodcuts of 1505 and Triumphal Imagery in Venetian Renaissance Books", in Grand Scale: Oversize and Composite Prints in the Age of Dürer and Titian, exhib. cat., ed. Larry Silver and Elizabeth Wycoff, Wellesley College, Davis Museum and Cultural Center; Yale University Art Gallery; Philadelphia Museum of Art (Seattle: Marquand Books, and New Haven: Yale University Press, 2008), 53–71. Not realizing that scholars writing in English were unaware of the Paris series, Monique Blanc published them without comment on the state in *Les Frises oubliées de Vélez Blanco*, exh. cat., Paris, Musée des Arts decoratifis, 1999, pp. 65–68, and figs. 9–12, 15–18, 21, and 23–25.

13. Bauer-Eberhardt, pp. 113–115; and Silvia Urbini, "Il Polifilo e gli altri libri figurati sul finire del Quattrocento," in *Verso il Polifilo*, pp. 49–78.

14. Lucian, *Opera*, Venice, Simone Bevilaqua for Benedetto Bordon, 25 August 1494 (Vienna: Österreichische Nationalbibliothek, Inc. 4.G.27, fol. 87 recto [m7 recto]). See Hermann J. Hermann, *Beschreibendes Verzeichnis der illuminierten Handschriften in Österreich*, VIII, Teil VI, *Die Handschriften und Inkunabeln der italienischen Renaissance*, 2: *Venetien* (Leipzig, 1931), 220–225 (No. 140), and pls. LXIX–LXXII; Fol. 87 is illustrated in color in Mariani Canova, *La miniature veneta*, Pl. 44.

15. Fol. a1 recto (HC 10261; E. 747; Sander 4037; illustrated in Essling, I, II, p. 210).

16. See note 14 above. Vienna, ÖNB, Inc. 4.G.27, fol. a2 recto (folio renumbered a2). Folios a1v–a2r are illustrated in color in Jonathan J. G. Alexander, ed., *The Painted Page: Italian Renaissance Book Illumination, 1450–1550* (London and Munich, 1994), p. 207. See discussions by Szépe, "The Book as Companion, The Author as Friend," pp. 80–81.

17. The request is reprinted and translated into English in Armstrong, "Benedetto Bordon, *Miniator*, pp. 90–91.

18. The fundamental tool for investigating Venetian books with woodcuts is the six-volume work by Victor Masséna, Prince d'Essling, *Les livres à figures Vénetiens de la fin du XVe siècle et du commencement du XVIe*, 6 vols. (Paris and Florence, 1907–14). Amplification and corrections to Essling appear in Max Sander, *Le livre à figures italien depuis 1467 jusqu'en 1530*, 6 vols. (Milan, 1942). See also Joseph Poppelreuter, *Der anonyme Meister des Poliphilo: Eine Studie zur italienischen Buchillustration und zur Antike in der Kunst des Quattrocento* (Strassburg: Heitz & Mündel, 1904).

I owe a special debt of thanks to Jonathan Alexander, who some years ago located a copy of Essling that I was able to acquire; in 1938, the copy of Essling was sold by Bernard Quaritch to Moses Marx, Esq., at Hebrew Union College, Cincinnati.

19. The books considered are either in Latin or in Italian translations from the Latin, but there are no texts printed in Greek. Combining entries from Essling and Sander, the authors and numbers of editions with woodcuts that were tabulated are: Aesop, 13; Apuleius, *Asinus Aur.*, 7; Caesar, 8; Catullus (Tibullus and Propertius), 1; Cicero (*De Officiis*, 6; *Epis. fam.*, 6; *De divina natura*, 1; *De Oratore*, 1; *Rhetorica*, 1; *Tusc. Quest.* 2); Diogenes Laertius, 1; Donatus, 5; Euclid, 3; Galen (*Recettario*), 7; Aulus Gellius, 2; Herodotus, 1; Horace, 5; Hyginus, 3; Juvenal, 8; Livy, 9; Lucan, 4; Lucian, 1; Macrobius, 3; Martial, 2; Ovid (*Metamorphoses*, 10; *Epis. Heroides*, 17; *De fastis*, 4; *De arte am.* and *De rem. amor.* 5; *Tristium*, 1); Persius, 5; Plautus, 2; Pliny, *Hist. nat.*, 5; Pliny the Younger, *Epis.* 1; Plutarch, *Vitae*, 5; Priscian, 1; Probus, 2; Ptolemy, *Geog.*, 1; Sallust, 8; Seneca,

Trag. 2; Strabo, 1; Suetonius, 2; Terence, 16; Valerius Maximus, 5; Virgil, 10; Vitruvius, 1.

20. Thus far I have been able to study the woodcuts of some 55 or (27 percent) of the 204 editions, looking at 26 of the 38 authors (68 percent) (July 7, 2005), trying in all cases to concentrate on the first appearance of a given cycle. Because of their rarity, I mention the libraries in which I have seen a given volume. These include Houghton Library of Harvard University (hereafter Houghton); the British Library (BL); the Biblioteca Casanatense, Rome; the Biblioteca Apostolica Vaticana (BAV); Biblioteca Nazionale Marciana in Venice (BNM).

21. Ovidius, *Epistolae Heroides,* Venice: Johannes Tacuinus, 10 July 1501 (E. 1136; Sander 5265; Houghton, TYP 525.01.663).

22. Ovidius, *Epistolae Heroides,* Venice, Bartholomaeus de Zanis, 10 June 1506 (E. 1138; Sander, 5267); reprinted by Bartolomaeus de Zanis, 20 December 1507 (E. 1139; Sander, 5268; Houghton, TYP 525.07.663F [Ruth Mortimer, *Harvard College Library Department of Printing and Graphic Arts, Catalogue of Books and Manuscripts.* Part II: *Italian 16th Century Books* (Cambridge, MA, 1974), 2 vols., no. 334]; BAV, Prop. Fide IV.19). Theseus and Ariadne appear on fol. h5 recto of the 1507 edition.

23. Images of the heroine writing are illustrated in Essling, I, II, pp. 428, 430, 433, and 435.

24. Virgil, *Opera,* Venice, Philippus Pintius, 15 September 1505 (Rome, Biblioteca Casanatense, P V. 2. CCC). Craig Kallendorf, *Bibliography of Venetian Editions of Virgil, 1470–1599, Biblioteca di Bibliografia italiana,* vol. 123 (Florence: Olschki, 1991), no. 44; and Kallendorf, *Virgil and the Myth of Venice (Oxford: Clarendon Press,* 1999), p. 158, and Pl. 5. The 1505 edition was unknown to Essling, who however published woodcuts from the subsequent 1508 edition, now known to have reemployed all twenty woodcuts from the 1505 one (Virgil, *Opera,* Venice, Bartholomaeus de Zannis, 3 August 1508 [Essling, 56; Sander 7653]). The 1508 Council of the Gods is illustrated in Essling I, I, p. 63. Bartholomaeus de Zannis reprinted the 1508 edition in 1510 (E. 57; Sander, 7654; Houghton, TYP 525.10.868F [Mortimer, 524]). Essling also knew the edition of 30 June 1507, printed by Bernardinus Stagninus (E. 55; Sander 7652; BAV, Prop. Fide III. 165), and he illustrated its woodcut of the Council of the Gods (Essling I, I, p. 61). Long ago, the 1507 image seemed to me to be an inferior copy of the 1508 woodcut, clearly a chronological impossibility unless there was an earlier edition. Kallendorf's illustration of the Council of the Gods from the 1505 edition in *Virgil and the Myth of Venice* led to the solution of this puzzle.

25. The full page from the 1510 edition is illustrated in Mortimer, p. 736.

26. See note 10 above.

27. London, British Library, Add. MS 11355, fol. 1r (Bauer-Eberhardt, fig. 1, and pp. 103, 106).

28. See David Wright, *The Roman Virgil and the Origins of Medieval Book Design* (London: British Library, 2001), esp. pp. 15, 62.

29. For example, the dogs in the foreground of the Annunciation in a *Book of Hours,* Houghton, MS *90M-16 (ex-Fogg Art Museum, 1930.306), fol. 14 verso; and in the Pentecost, one of four detached miniatures from a *Book of Hours,* New York, Pierpont Morgan Library, MS 369, fol. 4.

30. *Graduale romanum,* Venice, LucAntonio Giunta, 1499–1501, Vol. II, fol. 220 (H. 7844; E. 1208; Sander, 3211; illustrated in Armstrong, "Bordon, Aldus, Giunta," fig. 14).

31. Horace, *Opera,* Venice, Donino Pintius, 5 February 1505 [1506], fols. 137v (r7 v) and 128 (q6 r) respectively (E. 1165; Sander, 3457; BAV, ex-Inc. Prop. Fide IV.35). Interestingly, Essling noted that these two woodcuts must have come from an unknown edition of Virgil. The date of 15 September 1505 for the newly recognized Virgil edition also means that the Horace date must be 5 February 1506 (not 1505), following Venetian usage of beginning the year on March 1.

32. Cicero, *De Officiis, De Amicitia, De Senectute, Paradoxa,* Venice, Johannes Tacuinus, 20 February 1506 [1507] (E. 9; Sander, 1966; Houghton, Lc 38.738*; BAV, Stamp. R.G.Classici II.33). See also E. 11–14 and Sander 1968–1970.

33. 1506 ed., fol. DD4 recto (fol. 208 recto); and 1501 ed. fol. a3 recto, respectively.

34. Fol. 25 recto (Essling, I, I, p. 34). For the text see also Cicero, *De Officiis,* Latin and English trans. by Walter Miller, Loeb Classical Library (Cambridge, MA: Harvard University Press, 1913), Book I, VIII, xiii.

35. Massing noted that the Triumph illustrating the chapter on Glory (fol. 124v) in this 1506 [1507] Cicero, *De officiis,* was the first known reflection of one woodcut from the Bordon/Jacob of Strassburg *Triumph of Caesar* (Woodcut "K"); he did not, how-

ever, take the next step of attributing the design of the *De officiis* woodcut to Bordon ("*The Triumph of Caesar* by Benedetto Bordon," pp. 18–19, n. 78).

36. *De officiis,* III, xxv.

37. *De officiis,* III, xxv.

38. I am grateful to Professor Szépe for this suggestion.

39. This phenomenon has been several times addressed by Jonathan J. G. Alexander. See his "Constraints on Pictorial Invention in Renaissance Illumination: The Role of Copying North and South of the Alps in the Fifteenth and Early Sixteenth Centuries," *Miniatura* 1 (1988): 123–35; and Jonathan J. G. Alexander, *Medieval Illuminators and Their Methods of Work* (New Haven, CT and London: Yale University Press, 1993), esp. chapter 6, pp. 121–49.

40. Juvenal, *Satirae,* Venice, Aldus Manutius, 1501 (Manchester, John Rylands University, 8666, inserted leaf verso, opposite fol. a2 recto). See Szépe, "The Book as Companion," pp. 86–88 and fig. 8; Szépe, "Modes of Illuminating Aldines," pp. 195–96; illustrated in color in Armstrong, *Studies,* Pl. XVI.

41. Juvenal, *Satirae,* no city or printer, 1503, fol. a1 recto (E. 787, illus. I, II, p. 235; Sander, 3732; Houghton, Inc. 5996.5, Lobby I.4.20); see Szépe as in note 40.

42. Fol. C6 recto (see note 8 above).

43. Fol. 24 verso; illustrated in Essling, I, I, p. 34.

44. *De officiis,* I, VII.

45. Plinius, *Historia naturalis,* Venice, Melchior Sessa, 20 August 1513 (E. 4; Sander, 5760; Houghton, Lp 27.109.7 F*; BL 442.h.2 (1); BNM, Rari V. 184). Interestingly, one woodcut designed for Book XXIX of the 1513 Pliny was reused on the title page of a Galen, *Recettario* printed 25 August 1520 by Alessandro and Benedetto Bindoni (Essling, no. 1601, II, I, p. 165, mistakenly cited the Galen with the date of 1510; the correct date is given by Sander, no. 3005). The woodcut shows a man having a poultice applied to his leg, a scene applicable the discussion of medical practices discussed by Pliny (illustrated in Essling, I, I, p. 30).

46. Pliny, *Natural History,* Latin and English trans. by H. Rackham, London, 1945, Book XIV, chap. XXVIII.

47. Plutarchus, *Vitae virorum illustrium,* Venice, Melchior Sessa and Vincenzo di Paolo, 26 November 1516, fol. 233 verso (E. 597; Sander, 5785; Houghton, WKR 14.2.4; BL 10604.K.6; BAV Prop. Fid. IV. 169; BNM, Rari V. 173).

48. Apuleius, *Asinus Aureus* (in Italian), Venice, Niccolò Zoppino and Vincenzo di Paolo, 10 September 1518 (E. 1325; Sander, 487; Houghton, TYP 525.18.255; BAV, Capponi VI.66; see also Sotheby's, New York, *The Collection of Otto Schäfer,* Part I, *Italian Books,* December 8, 1994, Lot 13).

49. For Bordon's Lucian, see above nn. 14–16. See further Lucian, [Works], 8 vols., London and New York: Loeb Classical Library, 1913 ff., vols. 1–5 translated into English by A. M. Harmon; vol. 6 trans. by K. Kilburn; vols. 7–8 trans. by M. D. Macleod.

50. Apuleius, *Opera,* Venice, Philippus Pintius, 16 September 1510 (E. 1323; Sander, 485; BAV Racc. Gen. Classici II.187).

51. Armstrong, "Bordon, Aldus, Giunta"; and Szépe, "Modes of Illuminating Aldines."

52. Armstrong, "Woodcuts for Liturgical Books."

53. Information from Helena K. Szépe, April 21, 2005. See especially Giordana Mariani Canova, "La decorazione dei documenti ufficiali in Venezia dal 1460 al 1530," *Atti del Istituto Veneto di scienze, lettere, ed arte* 126 (1968–69): 319–34; and Helena K. Szépe, *Venetian Manuscripts and Myths of State* (book nearing completion).

54. *Evangeliarium for Santa Giustina, Padua,* 1523–25 (Dublin, Chester Beatty Library, MS W. 107, folios partially dismounted). (See *The Painted Page,* cat. no. 118, with further bibliography).

55. In his first will Bordon left his astronomical and philosophical books to his humanist son who had received a *laurea* from the University of Padua. Billanovich transcribes two wills made by Bordon (pp. 250–53), the first of which also shows that Bordon had business dealings with Nicolo Zoppino, printer of the 1518 Apuleius.

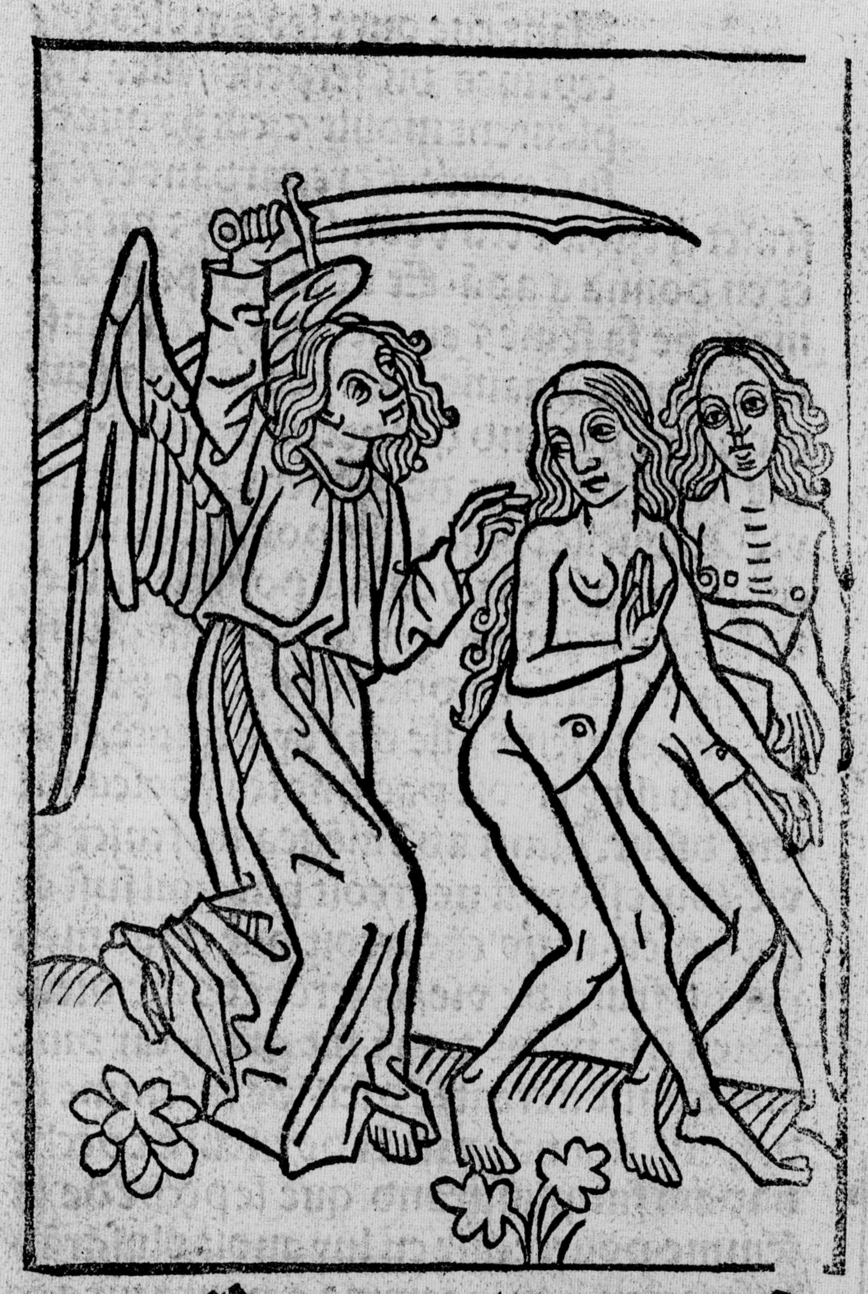

Pres ce que adam ꝛ eue eurẽt mẽge du fruict ꝺ vie / leurs yeulx furẽt ouuers et ꝯgneurent

Peter Stallybrass

Image against Text: On Not Reading Genesis

Who does not know the story of Adam and Eve? In Genesis, their expulsion from Eden goes something like this: Adam and Eve eat the forbidden apple, they become suddenly aware of their nakedness, and they try to hide their genitals with fig leaves. But God is not deceived and casts them out of Eden. To prevent their returning, he places St. Michael with a flaming sword at the gates of Paradise. One of the ways in which this story was spread in fifteenth- and sixteenth-century Europe was through the circulation of thousands of woodcuts and engravings in printed books. Few parts of the biblical narrative were more frequently represented—and this part had the great advantage of appearing where most people were likely to read or to see: the beginning. Given the combination of image and text—image and *sacred* text—in illustrated Bibles, it would seem reasonable to assume that the woodcuts are closely related to the passages that they illustrate. My question here addresses only a single aspect of a single moment of the story: what were Adam and Eve wearing when they were expelled?

A series of elegantly simple woodcuts in a 1483 *Speculum,* printed in Lyon, condenses the crucial moments of the third chapter of Genesis.[1] One depicts Adam and Eve naked in front of the Tree of Knowledge, Eve offering the apple to Adam. A second shows St. Michael, sword raised, expelling the couple from Paradise (fig. 1). A third shows Adam and Eve, now clothed, working outside Eden, Adam tilling the ground with a hoe while Eve spins, a baby at her breast. The consequences of the Fall are here sharply captured: the gendered division of labor, Adam digging and Eve spinning; the double labor which Eve now performs (spinning and giving birth to children); and the clothing of Adam and Eve, here in garments that are clearly differentiated by

Fig. 1. St. Michael expelling Adam and Eve from Paradise. *Speculum humanae salvationis.* Lyons, 1483 (Rosenwald Collection 383, Library of Congress, Washington).

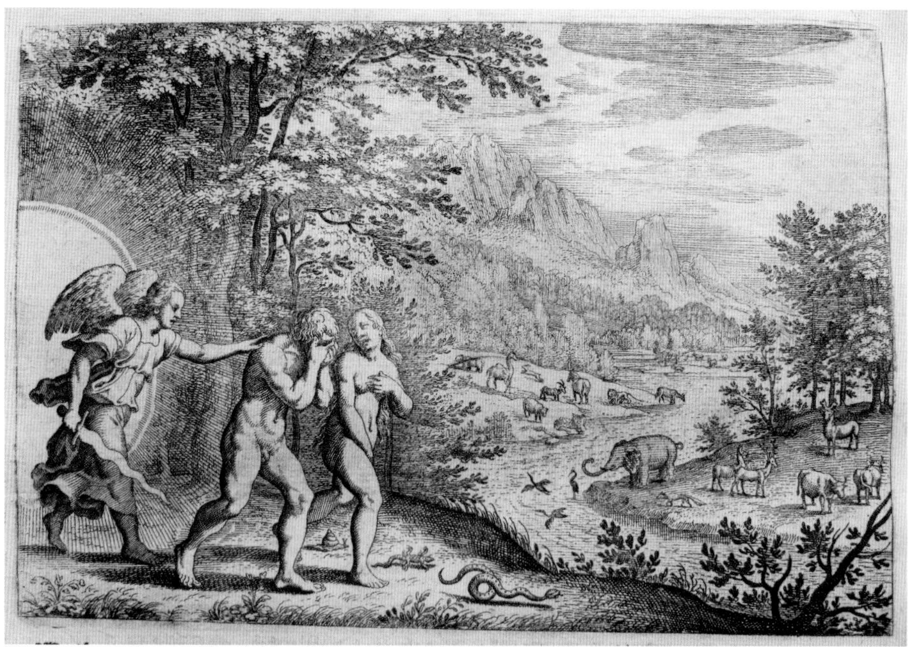

Fig. 2. The Expulsion from Paradise, engraving by Matthäus Merian. *Biblia,* Frankfurt, 1704 (Mortimer Rare Book Room, Smith College).

gender, Eve in a long robe, Adam in a smock with his hose rolled down to below his knees. Adam and Eve, then, are naked when they are cast out, and it is only after their expulsion that they are clothed.

Half a century earlier, in 1426–27, Masaccio painted in the Brancacci Chapel in Florence a fresco of the expulsion. Masaccio depicted Michael flying above Adam and Eve as he expels them. Adam and Eve are naked. Adam's genitals are displayed to the viewer; Eve, on the other hand, tries to hide her nakedness, her left hand covering her genitals, her right hand covering her breasts. The painting had an extraordinary afterlife, being imitated by Raphael, Michelangelo, Giulio Romano, and many other artists. And adaptations circulated widely through woodcuts and engravings. In the 1630s, for instance, Mattäus Merian copied Romano's version of the naked Adam, his head in his hands, his genitals exposed, in an engraving that was used in many Lutheran Bibles (fig. 2). Merian's plate was itself repeatedly reused (as late as a 1704 Frankfurt Bible) and in turn provided a model that was copied and adapted.[2]

Woodcuts by Dürer and Holbein popularized other iconographies of the expulsion. In Dürer's expulsion in the *Small Passion* of 1510, in contrast to Masaccio's, Eve stands in front of Adam, partly obscuring his naked genitals (fig. 3).[3] Her back is

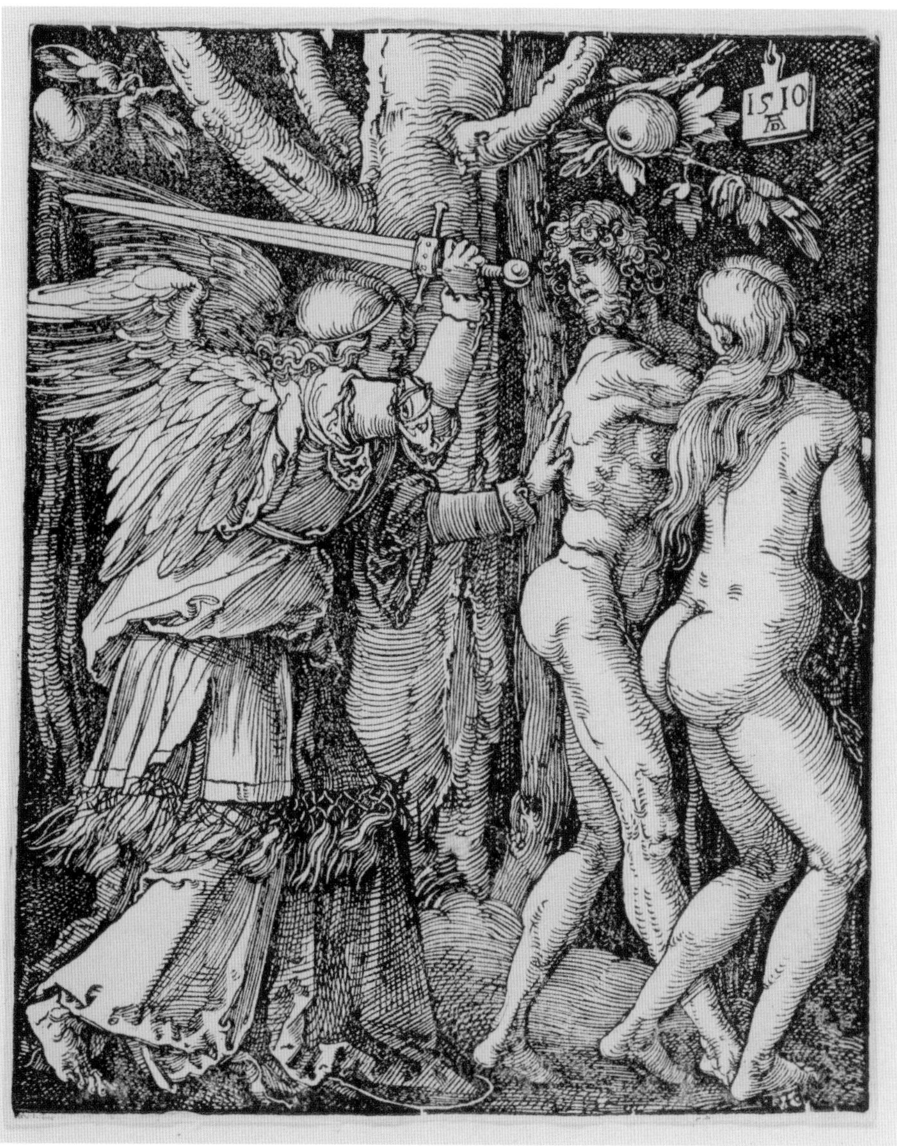

Fig. 3. The Expulsion from Paradise, woodcut by Albrecht Dürer. Nuremberg, 1510 (Prints and Photographs Division LC-USZC4-13353, Library of Congress, Washington).

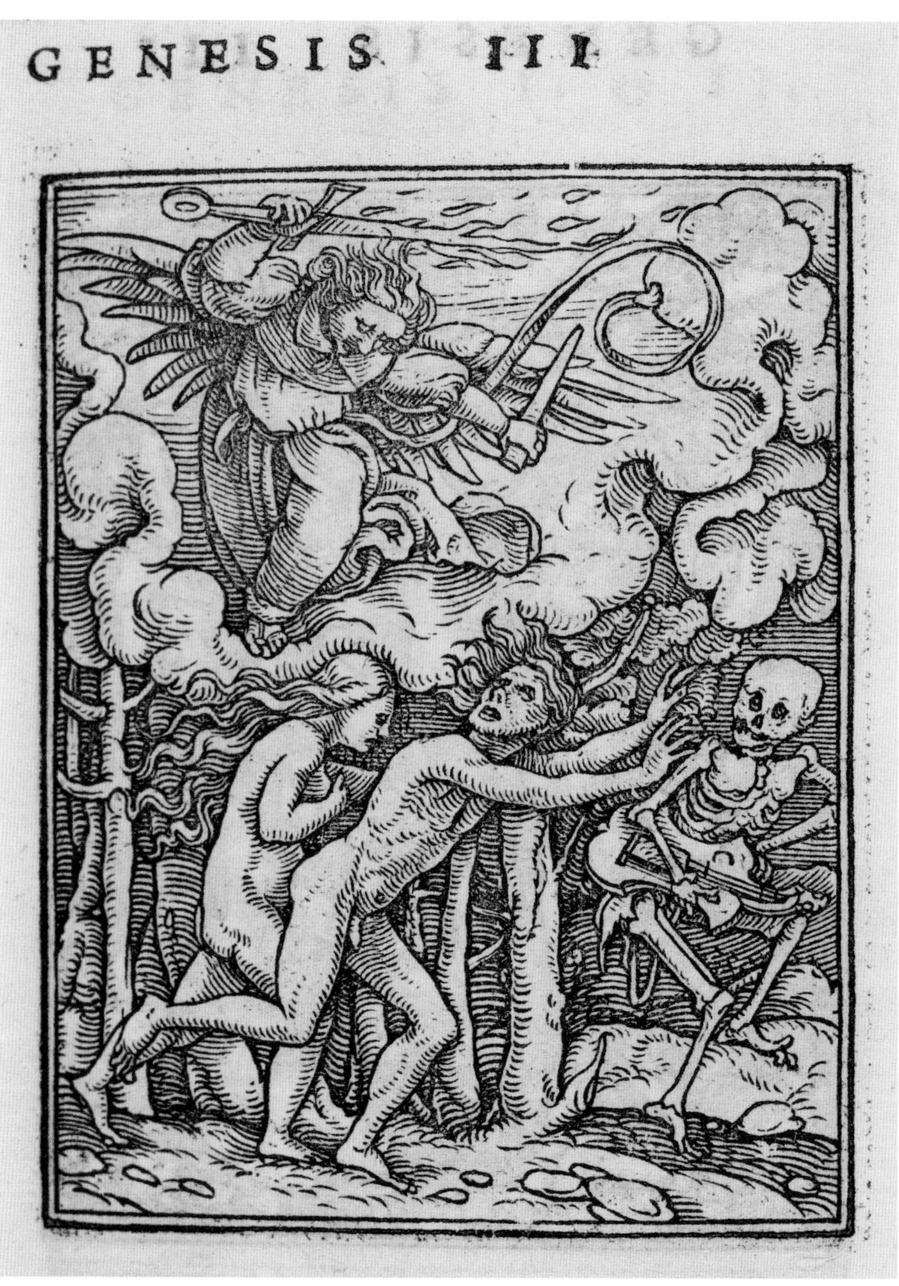

Fig. 4. Adam and Eve, woodcut by Hans Holbein. *Les simulachres & historiees faces de la Mort, avtant elegamm̄et pourtraictes, que artificiellement imaginées.* Lyon, [M. et G. Trechsel] 1538 (Rosenwald Collection 1010, Library of Congress, Washington).

turned away, whereas Masaccio's Eve is half-turned to the viewer. And while Masaccio's Adam and Eve face forward, Adam's head in his hand, Dürer's couple turn their heads back to look at Michael's raised sword. As with Masaccio's painting, versions of Dürer's woodcut were widely disseminated. In his 1529 Latin Bible, Jean Crespin included a composite cut of Genesis 3, on the left of which Adam and Eve stand in front of the Tree of Knowledge, about to eat the apple.[4] Even before the Fall, they are covering themselves with fig leaves, strikingly depicted as if they were fans at the end of wooden handles. But on the right, their postures imitated from Dürer, Adam and Eve are now naked as they are cast out.

Holbein's design for the expulsion, cut by Hans Lützelburger for the Dance of Death series, first appeared in Lyon in 1538 (fig. 4).[5] Holbein emphasizes the connection between the naked body and the nakedness of death. Holbein's trees, in contrast to Merian's, are bare, perhaps dead, and there is no sign of the rich animal life (including elephants and camels) that inhabit the new world toward which Merian's Adam and Eve go. Holbein also includes the skeletal figure of Death, who recalls the further "undressing" that awaits the banished couple: as they are now stripped of their fig leaves, Death will later strip them of their flesh.

Holbein's cuts of the Dance of Death were immensely popular throughout the sixteenth century. Four of Holbein's illustrations for the Dance of Death were further disseminated when they were included a year later in an illustrated version of the Old Testament, *Historiarum Veteris Instrumenti Icones ad Viuum Expressae.*[6] The designs for the book were accompanied by brief "expositions" of the relevant biblical texts. These expositions were first printed in Latin and French, but they were later translated into other vernaculars. In 1549, Jean Frellon, one of the brothers who had printed the first edition of the *Icones* in Lyon, published in the same city *The images of the Old Testament, lately expressed: set forthe in Ynglishe and Frenche, with a playn and brief exposition.* The bizarre "Ynglishe" that accompanies the cut of the expulsion reads:

> Vuhen [i.e., when] Adam and Heua dyd atknolege thor syn, they dyd fle from the face of God, and ar obiected vnto deth. Cherubim is seth lefore [i.e., before] paradise of plesur vuyth [i.e., with] a fyrey svourd.[7]

Copies and adaptations of Masaccio, Dürer, and Holbein were increasingly used to illustrate Bibles and biblical abridgements. And for all the iconographic differences between the artists, they agreed in one thing: when Adam and Eve were expelled, they were naked.

But *were* they? Didn't Adam and Eve cover their genitals with fig leaves? Were they still wearing those fig leaves when they were expelled? In 1483, Anton Koberger

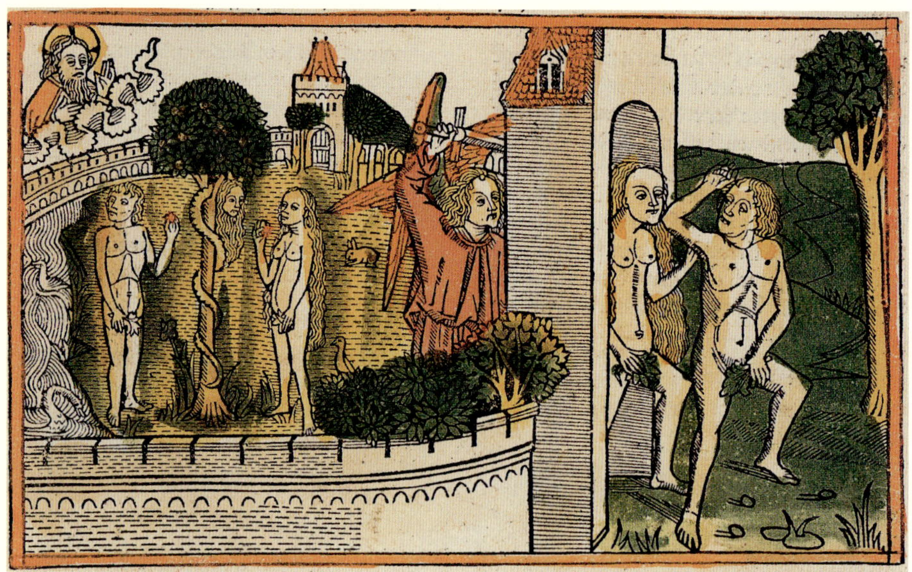

Fig. 5. The Fall of Adam and Eve. *Biblia,* Nuremberg, Anton Koberger, 17 February 1483 (Rosenwald Collection 93, Library of Congress, Washington).

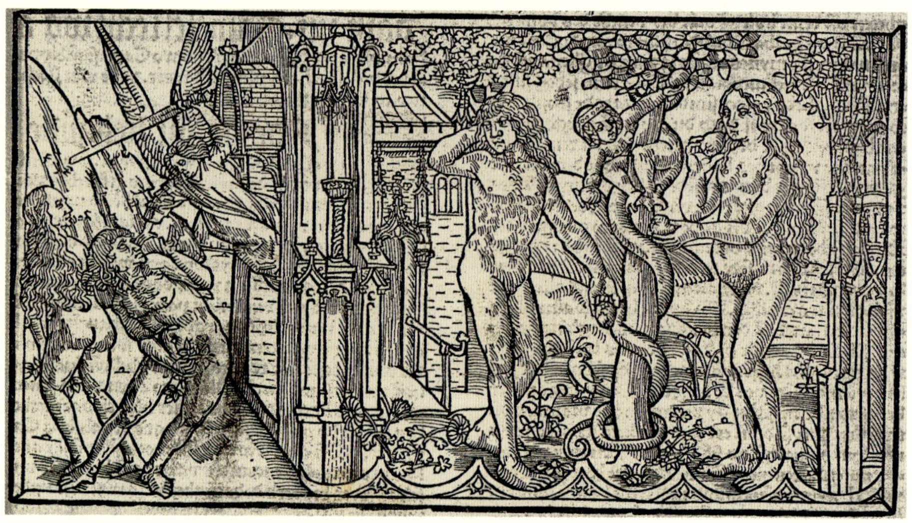

Fig. 6. The Fall of Adam and Eve. *Biblia.* Lübeck, Steffen Arndes, 1494 (Rosenwald Collection 168, Library of Congress, Washington).

published the Nuremberg Bible, for which he reused the woodcuts from a German Bible printed by Heinrich Quentell c. 1478. In the cut of the Fall, Adam and Eve hold fig leaves over their genitals not only before the Fall but also as they are expelled (fig. 5).[8] The Rosenwald copy has been hand-colored, the coloring drawing particular attention to the green fig leaves. In the 1494 Lübeck Bible, there is, as in the Nuremberg Bible, a double scene of the eating of the fruit and of the expulsion. Adam and Eve are here naked as they eat the fruit, but they have nonetheless acquired leaves to hide their nakedness as they cower outside the gates of Eden (fig. 6).[9]

So when they were expelled, were Adam and Eve naked or did they each cover their genitals with a fig leaf? In 1493, a decade after publishing the Nuremberg Bible, Anton Koberger printed his most famous book: the Nuremberg Chronicle. Among the splendid cuts by Michael Wolgemut and Wilhelm Pleydenwurff that Koberger commissioned for the project is a large illustration of the expulsion (fig. 7).[10] The size of the cut allowed for a virtuoso display not only of Gothic architecture but of exotic trees in an attempt to give historical authenticity to the Chronicle's version of Paradise.

But there is further evidence of the care with which these cuts were made. As in the Nuremberg and Lübeck Bibles, Adam and Eve are holding fig leaves in the Chronicle, but there is a significant difference. The Chronicle's couple, both as they eat the apples and as they are cast out, hold *bundles of leaves* that have been *tied together* (fig. 7). Each bundle has two small cords around the stems of the leaves. Michael Wolgemut may also have been the maker of a cut of Adam and Eve that Koberger had used two years previously in his edition of Stephan Fridolin's *Schatzbehalter der wahren Reichtümer des Heils.* In the *Schatzbehalter,* as in the Chronicle, the stems of the leaves are tied together with cords (fig. 8).[11]

So if Adam and Eve were wearing anything, were they wearing detached leaves or leaves tied together in bundles? I have deliberately refrained from referring to any textual account of the expulsion not only to emphasize the exegetical work that the images do but also to suggest that it is the visual rather than the textual tradition through which we still usually "read" the story of Adam and Eve.

As to the question of detached fig leaf or fig leaves tied together, the biblical text (3:7) is quite explicit:

> And the eyes of them both were opened, & they knew that they were naked, and they *sewed figge leaues together*...[12] [my emphasis]

In other words, Adam and Eve don't disguise themselves by each wearing a single fig leaf; they *manufacture* the world's first form of clothing. Sewing is indeed their first labor, since before the Fall they didn't have to work. So the original profession of

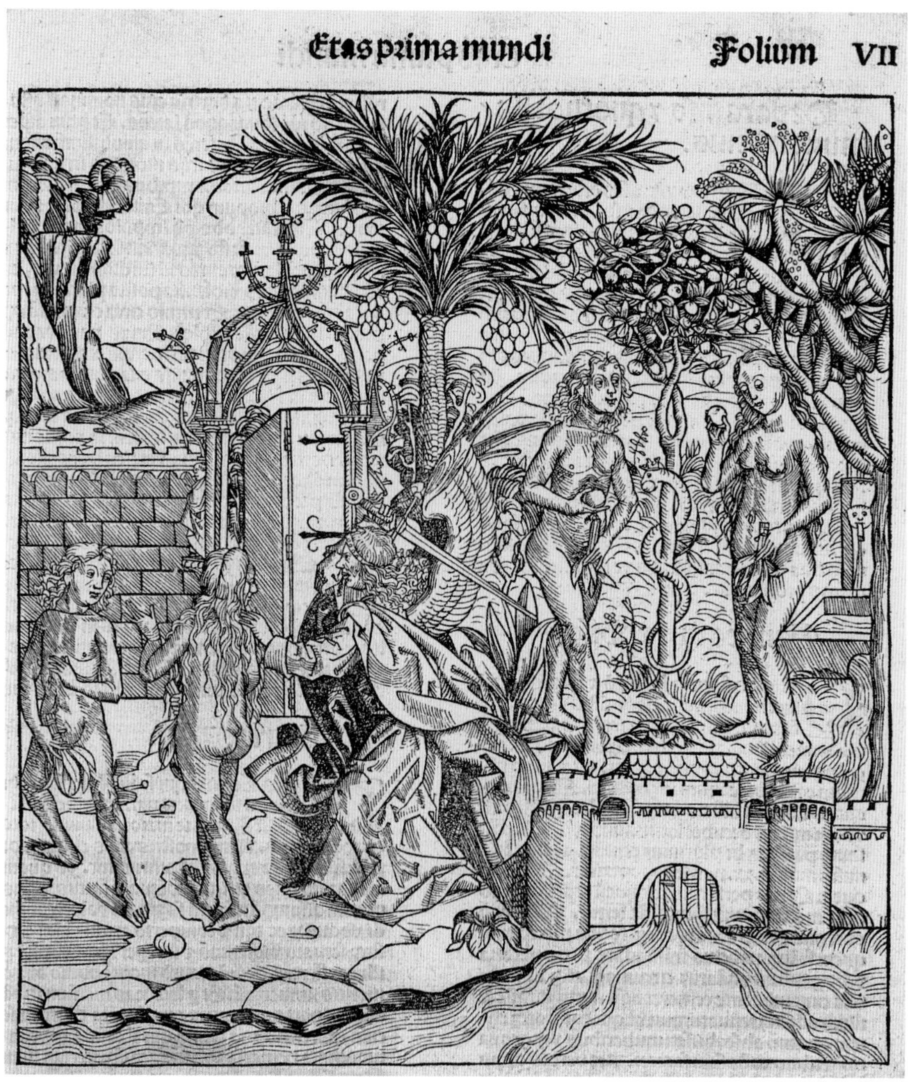

Figs. 7. Expulsion of Adam and Eve. Schedel, Hartmann. *Lib[er] cronicarum, cu[m] figuris et ymagi[ni]bus ab inicio mu[n]di.* Nuremberg, Anton Koberger, 12 July 1493 (Rosenwald Collection 163, Library of Congress, Washington).

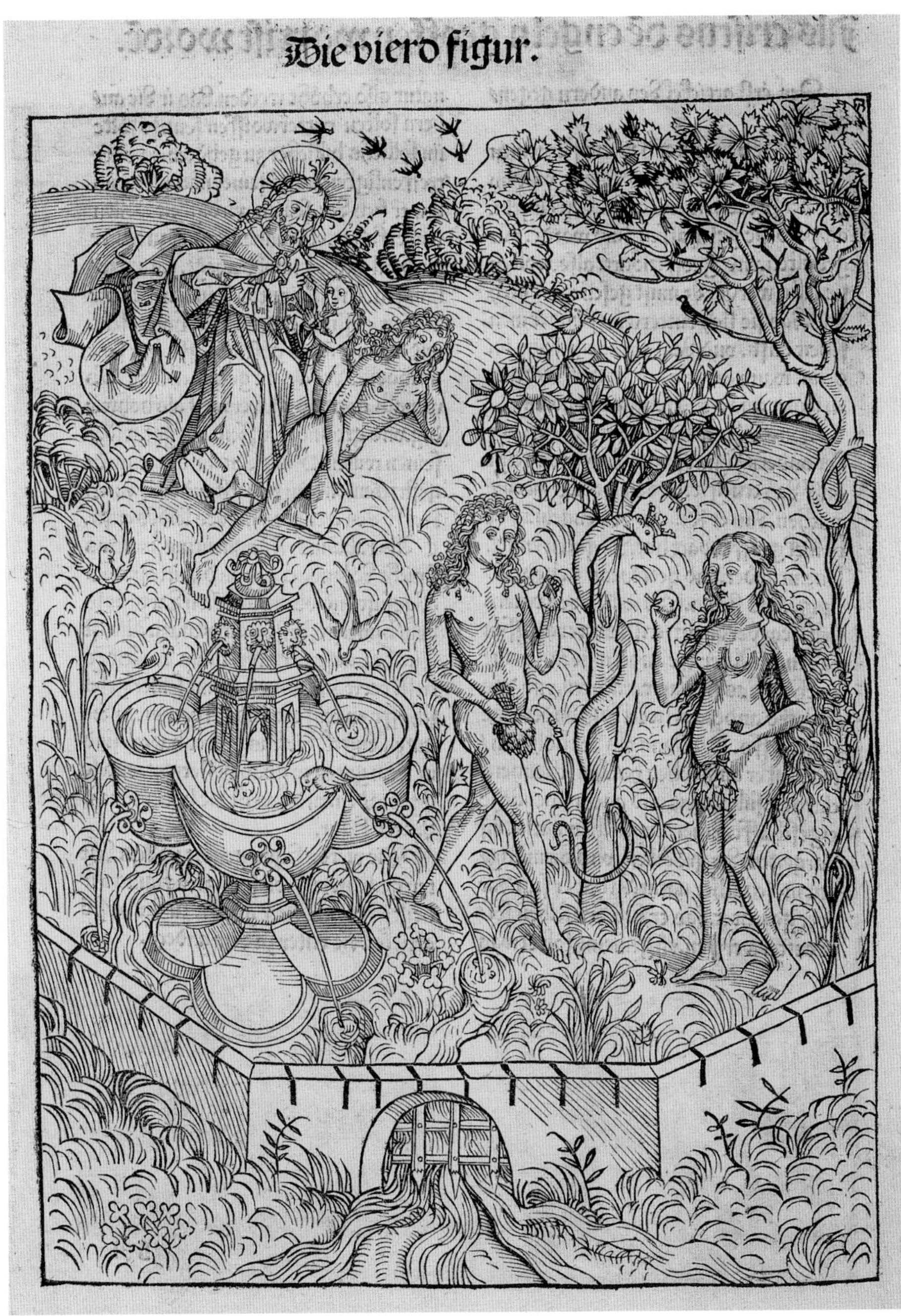

Fig. 8. Adam and Eve. Fridolin, Stephan. *Schatzbehalter der wahren Reichtümer des Heils.* Nuremberg, Anton Koberger, 1491 (Rosenwald Collection 154, Library of Congress, Washington).

men and women is tailoring.[13] The fact that Adam and Eve sew seems to have been of more interest to Renaissance readers than that they wore fig leaves. Nicholas Gibbens reproved the many people who asked "where *Adam* had a thread to sew his figge-leaves."[14] And when in 1630 an Essex minister preached a sermon about Adam and Eve making themselves coats of fig leaves, "a critical parishioner demanded to know where they got the thread to sew them with."[15]

It is striking that this detail of the sewing together of the fig leaves scarcely appears in visual representations. Artists had to choose which aspects of the biblical story to represent, and this was not one they chose. Even when artists did depict Adam and Eve's tailored garments, there was the further problem of how to depict them. In the cuts for Koberger's *Schatzbehalter* and Nuremberg Chronicle, Adam and Eve have to use their hands to hold their new form of clothing in place. In both the 1608 and the 1616 copies of Thomas Trevilian's commonplace book, the biblical text of Genesis 3:27 is accompanied by paintings of Adam and Eve holding fig leaves in their hands. But in the previous images, when they are discovered by God, they are wearing self-supporting girdles of leaves.[16] Similarly, the expelled couple in Jan Wierix's engraving wear leaves that are tied together around the middle of their bodies.[17] Both Wierix and the maker(s) of Trevilian's books are responding to a part of the biblical text that I did not quote before. In full, Genesis 3:27 reads:

> And the eyes of them both were opened, & they knew that they were naked, and they sewed figge leaues together, *and made themselues aprons.* [my emphasis]

That is the King James version, but in the earlier Geneva translation, Adam and Eve "sewed figtre leaues together, and made them selues *breeches* [my emphasis]."[18] This odd choice of word led to the Geneva Bible being known as the "Breeches Bible," the translation of this single verse giving the name for the whole Bible. The translation is so striking because breeches were specifically gendered male. Indeed, breeching was the crucial rite of passage through which a boy, who had previously worn skirts, put on the attire of a man. So what did it mean to say that Eve wore breeches?

The gendering of Adam and Eve's clothes had long been a problem for Jewish and Christian exegetes alike. Rabbi Abba bar Kahana, for instance, wrote:

> What is not written is "an apron," but rather "aprons."
>
> C. The sense of the plural is this: a variety of clothing, such as shirts, robes, and linen cloaks.
>
> D. And just as these sorts of garments are made for a man, so for a woman they make girdles, hats, and hair nets.[19]

Rabbi Kahana's Adam and Eve already obey the prohibition of Deuteronomy, which dictates that men's and women's clothes must be distinct from each other—in other words, a woman must never put on breeches. So in this exegesis, Adam and Eve are hard at work producing *gendered* clothing: shirts and cloaks for a man; girdles, hats, and hair nets for a woman. But the gendered distinctions that Rabbi Kahana attempts to establish find support neither in the biblical text nor in the dominant iconographic traditions, which depicted Adam and Eve naked, or each holding a single leaf or with bunches of leaves tied together, or with girdles of leaves.

If the illustrations of Genesis 3:7 converged on giving an ungendered depiction of Adam and Eve's clothes, they diverged radically in what clothing, if any, they gave to Adam and Eve at the expulsion. In the representations of the couple's clothing that I have analyzed to this point, Adam and Eve are depicted one of the four following ways:

1. Naked
2. Holding single fig leaves or twigs
3. Holding fig leaves tied together
4. Wearing self-supporting girdles of leaves

The simple and astonishing fact remains that all four of these ways of depicting the expulsion directly contradict the text that they supposedly illustrate. In Genesis 3:21, two verses *before* Adam and Eve are cast out of Eden, God reclothes them:

> Vnto Adam also, and to his wife, did the LORD God make coates of skinnes, and clothed them.

From the perspective of the textual tradition that the images supposedly illustrate, every image that I have examined so far is textually wrong. Far from illustrating the text, these images materialize counter-narratives that contradict not only God's word but also his actions. To make this point, I have had to suppress the fact that throughout the Middle Ages there was an iconographic tradition that drew particular attention to God's reclothing of Adam and Eve. Among the greatest representations of the expulsion are the thirteenth-century mosaics in San Marco (themselves based on the fifth-century Cotton manuscript).[20] The part of the Genesis story from the creation of Eve to the expulsion is divided up into ten segments, three of which are composite. In the mosaics, Adam and Eve eat the fruit and gather leaves together (although the act of sewing is not shown). They are then discovered and admonished by God (in his person as the Son), who pronounces sentence upon them as they kneel, now naked again, in front of him. God then reclothes them in robes made of animal skins. It is only after he has reclothed them that God himself casts them out. (St. Michael does not appear in this version of the story, although a fiery cherubim is depicted behind God.)

At the moment of their expulsion, the San Marco Adam and Eve are wearing identical robes; indeed, it would be almost impossible to tell them apart were it not for the fact that Adam is carrying a hoe and Eve a distaff. It is true that Eve's hair is slightly longer, but both figures are beardless and breastless (although Eve had previously been distinguished by small breasts). Only after the expulsion, where Eve appears seated and holding a distaff, is she depicted as a mother with "fallen" breasts. Before the Fall, she had no need for her breasts, since it is only after the expulsion that Adam and Eve are told, in partial recompense for their mortality, to be fruitful and multiply.

A less well known version of God's redressing of Adam and Eve appears on three panels of a Spanish reliquary made in Léon in about 1063.[21] In the first of these panels, God reprimands Adam ("Dixit Deus, Adam, Ubi Es"), while Adam clutches a fig leaf in one hand and with the other points the finger of blame at Eve, who in turn points the finger of blame at the serpent (or perhaps they both point at the serpent). In the wonderful second panel, God, who has already clothed Eve, puts a tunic over Adam, whose head just peeps through the neck-opening. In the third panel, Michael expels the fully clothed couple, whose hands point toward the world in which they will now have to make their way.

From the Church Fathers to the Reformation and Counter-Reformation, it was God's reclothing of Adam and Eve, not the fig leaves behind which Adam and Eve previously hid, that was the primary focus of biblical exegesis. Asserting their independence from God even as they felt shame, Adam and Eve made their own vegetable clothes. In clothing themselves, they claimed self-ownership (in our society it is above all children and prisoners who, not owning themselves, are clothed by others). But God does not allow Adam and Eve to clothe themselves. Claiming them as his subjects, he strips them of the clothes that they have made and reclothes them in his livery. According to Luther, God, by reclothing Adam and Eve in the skins of dead animals, introduces death into Eden even before the Fall. Why? As a memory system. For Luther, clothing is a memorial of death:

> *Unto Adam also and to his wife did the Lord God make coats of skins, and clothed them* (3:21). God clothed them with skins of slain animals to remind them that they were mortal and lived in (*constant*) danger of death.[22]

Death is the consequence of the Fall, and the mind alone is not an adequate tool for remembering that terrible fate. If mourning clothes materialize the death of the beloved daily upon one's own body, acting as a bodily memory system, God will dress his servants in mourning clothes so as to mark their own deaths through the deaths of the animals they wear.

Calvin similarly argues that God reclothed Adam and Eve in animal skins "because their garmentes being made of that matter, they rather sauoured of that which was beastlie, then of skinne, or of wooll/ . . . and so to remember sinne."[23] And sin leads to death. As Gervase Babington argues, following Luther and Calvin, the clothing that Adam and Eve wear materially prefigures their own deaths:

> *God made Adam and his Wife coates of Skinnes.* The beginning of apparrell is heere to bee noted, that it was when wee had sinned, and so is vnto vs at this daye no otherwise, then if an offender should weare an halter all his life in remembrance of his fault.[24]

Clothes are thus, according to Babington, a rope around one's neck, permanently inscribing upon the wearer the sentence of death that has already been pronounced.

However, there was a counter-tradition according to which the skins that Adam and Eve put on prefigure Christ. As Abraham Rosse wrote in 1626:

> [Adam] had need of clothing, both for his body, which now was to be subiect to infirmities, as also for his soule, which now was defiled with sinne, and therefore must bee clothed with the righteousnesse of Christ; which garment hee did put on by beleeuing that Christ, the Lambe of GOD should be killed to clothe his naked soule, as this beast was killed to clothe his naked bodie.[25]

The first Adam puts on the second Adam (Christ, the sacrificial Lamb) in the figure of the animal skins in which God reclothes him. It is this tradition that Milton draws upon in *Paradise Lost,* where Christ

> pittying how they stood
> Before him naked to the aire, that now
> Must suffer change . . .
> As Father of his Familie he clad
> Thir nakedness with Skins of Beasts . . .
> Nor hee thir outward onely with the Skins
> Of Beasts, but inward nakedness, much more
> Opprobious, with his Robe of righteousness,
> Araying cover'd from his Fathers sight.[26]

Milton, reworking the exegetical tradition, twists it in a curious direction. Christ reclothes Adam and Eve in "his Robe of righteousness" so as to *hide* them from his Father's (i.e. God's) sight. Christ thus appears to side with, and even to imitate, the fallen couple against his Father.

If textual exegesis was attentive to the reclothing of Adam and Eve before the expulsion, visual exegesis was not. God's redressing of the fallen couple did not disappear altogether from visual representation but it was attenuated even when represented. Claude Paradin's *The true and lyuely historyke purtreatures of the vvoll Bible,* printed in Lyon in 1553, followed the model of Holbein's *Icones,* published in the same city in 1538, with each page consisting of a woodcut and a short expository text. The text of the expulsion reads (in English as eccentric as that in the *Icones*):

> God eche of them with a garment of skinne
> Clothed, driueth out the faire place of pleasure:
> Then of the frute the waikipeth [*sic*] Cherubin:
> Wherfore with death pursued are anon sure.[27]

The one clear part of this passage is the statement that God clothed each of them "with a garment of skinne."

In Bernard Salomon's accompanying cut (fig. 9), Adam and Eve are wearing cloaks of some kind. In contrast to the tunics in the Spanish reliquary, these garments billow open, providing little in the way of protection or warmth. The design on a majolica plate made in Urbino around 1570 is directly taken from Salomon's cut of the expulsion.[28] Adam's pink cloak on the plate shows that the garments in Salomon's cut looked more like cloth than animal skins. The plate also draws attention to the fact that Salomon's design combines the new cloak that God has given Eve with her own girdle of leaves, the green of the leaves standing out clearly against Eve's pink flesh on the plate. But even such attenuated images of God's act of reclothing are exceptional. In illustrations for Bibles, Adam and Eve are most often represented as naked.

In 1538, Thomas Cromwell, in his role as Henry VIII's vice-regent, ordered every clergyman to "set vp" the Great Bible that was then being printed "in some conuenient place wythin the said church that ye haue cure of, where as your parishioners may most com[m]odiously resorte to the same and reade it."[29] The State thus at first intended to make this book available to every parishioner in England and Wales. After the Bible was published in 1539, parishioners were not only able to read it (if they were literate) or to hear others read it aloud; they could also look at the many cuts in it. In the column for Genesis 3, the text reads:

> Vnto the same Adam also and to his wife did the Lord God make lethren garments, and clothed them . . .[30]

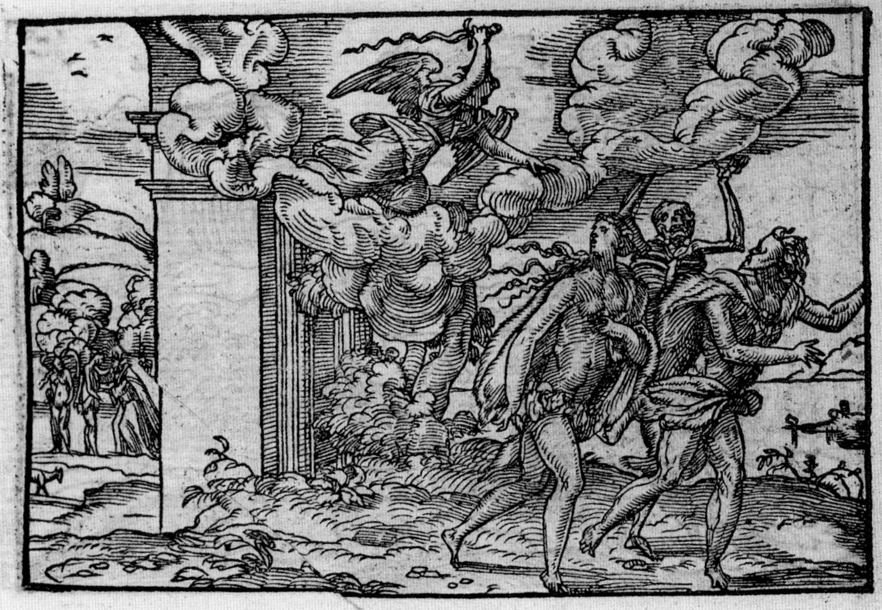

Fig. 9. Adam and Eve wearing cloaks, woodcut by Bernard Salomon. Borluut, Willem, *Historiarum memorabilium ex Exodo.* Lyons, Jean de Tournes, 1558. (Rosenwald Collection 1062, Library of Congress, Washington).

Five lines below, the text is interrupted by a cut that occupies the whole column (fig. 10). The last words above the cut are, "And the Lorde God sent..." Below the cut, the text continues, "them furth from the garde[n] of Eden..." In the cut that interrupts the text, the familiar figure of a winged and clothed St. Michael, with sword held aloft, pursues the fleeing Adam and Eve. They are naked. The image thus flies directly in the face of the text, which tells us that only after God has reclothed them were Adam and Eve expelled.

Images have played an important, sometimes a central, role in the interpretation of the Bible. Iconographic interpretation, to which Panofsky lent his massive erudition, has usually asserted that the meaning of Christian images could be deduced from Christian

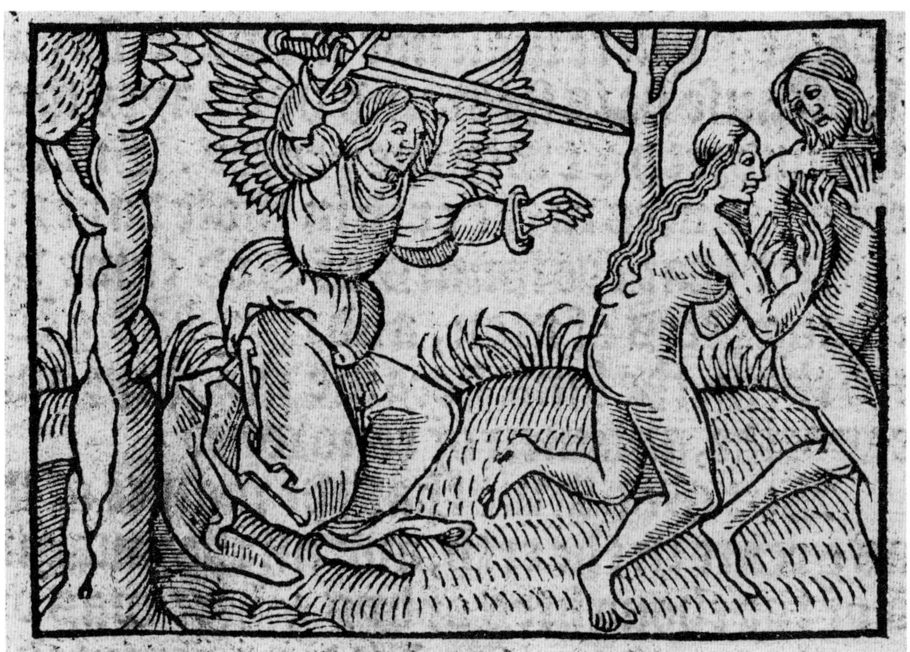

Fig. 10. St. Michael pursues fleeing Adam and Eve. *The Byble in Englyshe: that is to saye the conte[n]t of al the Holy Scrypture, both of ye Olde, and Newe Testame[n]t, with a prologe therinto / made by the reuerende father in God, Thomas Archbysshop of Cantorbury,* London, Edward Whytchurche, 1540 (Rare Book Collection BS160 1540, Library of Congress, Washington).

texts. In the third volume of his great work *Religious Art in France,* first published in 1908, Emile Mâle writes:

> there is not a single artistic work produced in the fifteenth century that cannot be explained by a book. The artists invented nothing: they translated into their own language the ideas of others.[31]

This is quite simply wrong.

Even where image follows text, there are important choices for the artist that usually have little or nothing to do with textual traditions. How to depict the fig leaves? How to clothe Adam and Eve? Is it God or St. Michael who casts Adam and Eve out, and if God, does he appear in the person of the Father or the Son? What kind of landscape are Adam and Eve entering? As I noted above, Holbein depicts bare or dead trees as the main element in his landscape, whereas Merian depicts a landscape teeming with animal and vegetable life. In the Folger's 1608 copy of Thomas Trevilian's commonplace book, corn (i.e., maize) grows on either side of Adam and Eve as they are expelled. Maize came only from the New World; even after it was imported to Europe and Asia, the plants themselves would have been visually legible almost entirely through images of the Americas. Adam and Eve, then, appear to have been cast out of Paradise and into the New World. In the Getty's 1616 copy of Trevilian's commonplace book, however, the artist takes a different approach to the scene. While the same image of Michael, Adam, and Eve appears, accompanied by the same text from Genesis, the maize has been replaced by two broccoli-like trees and an irruption of giant carnations which, like tulips, were being expensively hybridized in the Low Countries during this period. Even in the simplest cuts, detail after detail, from the positions of Adam and Eve's hands to the style of Michael's sword, had to be decided with little or no help from the biblical or any other text.

At the same time, every artist faced the problem of how to divide the text into visual segments. On the one hand, they could flesh out a scene by adding interpretive or decorative elements that are not in the text. On the other, they could condense several narrative moments into a single image. Such condensation is surely part of the explanation for the nakedness of Adam and Eve in many expulsion scenes. Nakedness conflates the Edenic state, the shame that follows the Fall, and the moment of expulsion, thus bringing together three moments into a single image. Such images also create counter-commentaries, though, that ignore or contradict the text. The most striking examples I know of images contradicting the text are the depictions of Adam and Eve naked or wearing only fig leaves as they are expelled from Eden.

If I was asked how I "knew" that Adam and Eve were either naked or wearing fig leaves at the expulsion, for most of my life I would have confidently responded that I had read the text. But I would have been wrong. In our "readings" of the expulsion of Adam and Eve from Paradise, the dominant visual traditions have massively outweighed the textual tradition. In my own "reading," without knowing it, I was attentively recalling not a written text but the paintings of Masaccio, Raphael, Michelangelo, and all the named and anonymous designers and makers of drawings, woodcuts, and engravings who followed not the text but each other. In other words, I have spent much of my life seeing, but not reading, Genesis. These visual exegeses are the more fascinating and important because they produce meanings for which there is no textual support.

NOTES

1. *Speculum* (Lyon, 1483), Rosenwald 383.

2. *Biblia* (Frankfurt, 1704), engravings by Matthew Mer[r]ian, Smith College: 220.53 1704.

3. Albrecht Dürer, The Expulsion from Paradise, from the *Kleine Passion* (Nuremberg?, 1510), Library of Congress, Woodcut, Prints and Photographs Division, 27.2.

4. *Textus Biblie* (Lyon: Jean Crespin, 1529), Folger Shakespeare Library 228–307f; *Biblia* (Lyon: Jean Crespin, 1540), Library of Congress BS75 1540 Bible Coll fol.

5. [Hans Holbein], *Les simulachres & historiees faces de la Mort, avtant elegamm et pourtraictes, que artificiellement imaginées* (Lyon, [M. et G. Trechsel] 1538), Library of Congress N7720.H6 A3 1538.

6. [Hans Holbein], *Historiarum Veteris Testamenti icones ad uiuum expressæ. Una cum breui . . . earundem & Latina & Gallica expositione* [The French verses by Gilles Corrozet.] (Lyon: M. and G. Trechsel, 1539).

7. [Hans Holbein], *The images of the Old Testament, lately expressed: set forthe in Ynglishe and Frenche, with a playn and brief exposition* (Lyon: Jean Frellon, 1549), STC 3045, sig. B.

8. *Biblia* (Nuremberg: Anton Koberger, 1483), Rosenwald 93, Rosenwald Coll folio.

9. *De Biblie* (Lübeck: Steffen Arndes, 1494), Incun. 1494 .B52 Rosenwald Coll.

10. *Lib[er] cronicarum, cu[m] figuris et ymagi[ni]bus ab inicio mu[n]di* (Nuremberg: Anton Koberger, 1493), Incun. 1493 .S3 Rosenwald Coll.

11. Stephan Fridolin, *Schatzbehalter der wahren Reichtümer des Heils* (Nuremberg: Anton Koberger, 1491), Rosenwald 140.

12. *The Holy Bible* [King James Bible] (London: Robert Barker, 1611), Genesis 3:7.

13. For a further discussion of this topic, see Ann Rosalind Jones and Peter Stallybrass, *Renaissance Clothing and the Materials of Memory* (Cambridge: Cambridge University Press, 2000), 269–77.

14. Nicholas Gibbens, *Questions and disputations concerning the holy Scripture* (London, 1601), 168–69.

15. Keith Tomas, *Religion and the Decline of Magic* (New York: Scribner, 1971), p. 161. I am indebted to Clare Costley for this reference.

16. Thomas Trevilian, *Commonplace Book, 1608,* Folger Shakespeare Library, V.b.232; Thomas Trevilian, *Commonplace Book, 1616,* Wormsley Library; and Nicholas Barker, *The Great Book of Thomas Trevilian: a Facsimile of the Manuscript in the Wormsley Library,* vol. 2 (London: Roxburghe Club, [2000]).

17. Jan Wierix, *The Expulsion from Paradise,* c. 1606, Cleveland Museum of Art 1994.16.

18. *The Bible* [The Geneva Bible] (Geneva: Rowland Hall, 1560), Genesis 3:21.

19. *Genesis Rabbah: the Judaic Commentary to the book of Genesis,* trans. Jacob Neusner (Atlanta, GA: Scholars Press, 1985).

20. See Otto Demus, *The Mosaics of San Marco in Venice,* 4 vols. (Chicago: University of Chicago Press, 1984), part 2, vol. 1, pp. 114–17, and part 2, vol. 2, color plate 32 and plates 121–30.

21. Reliquary of San Isidore, Real Colegiata de San Isidore, Spain, c. 1063. See David Simon, "Late Medieval Art in Spain," in *The Art of Medieval Spain* (New York: Metropolitan Museum of Art, 1993), no. 110, pp. 239–43.

22. Martin Luther, *Luther's Commentary on Genesis,* trans. J. Theodore Mueller, vol. 1 (Grand Rapids, Michigan: Zondervan, 1968), 85.

23. John Calvin, *A Commentarie of John Caluine, vpon the first booke of Moses,* trans. Thomas Tymme (London, 1578), 118–19.

24. Gervase Babington, *Certaine Plaine, briefe, and comfortable Notes vpon euerie Chapter of Genesis* (London, 1592), f. 21.

25. Abraham Rosse, *An Exposition on the Fourteene first Chapters of Genesis* (London, 1626), 69–70.

26. John Milton, *Paradise Lost. A Poem in Twelve Books. The Author John Milton. The Second Edition Revised and Augmented by the same Author* (London: S. Simmons, 1674), Book X, lines 211–23, pp. 257–58.

27. Claude Paradin, *The true and lyuely historyke*

purtreatures of the vvoll Bible (Lyon: Jean de Tournes, 1553), Library of Congress, BS1235 .P33 Rosenwald Coll, sig. B2.

28. Majolica plate, made in Urbino c. 1570, Scuole San Rocco, Inv. 16/c.

29. A. S. Herbert, *Historical Catalogue of Printed Editions of the English Bible 1525–1961* (London: the British and Foreign Bible Society, 1968), 25. See also J. F. Mozley, *Coverdale and His Bibles* (Lutterworth, 1953), 261.

30. *The Byble in Englyshe* (London: Edward Whytchurche, 1540), Library of Congress BS160 1540 (Office).

31. Emile Mâle, *Religious Art in France: The Late Middle Ages,* trans. Marthiel Matthews, Bollingen Series XC.3 (Princeton: Princeton University Press, 1986), vi.

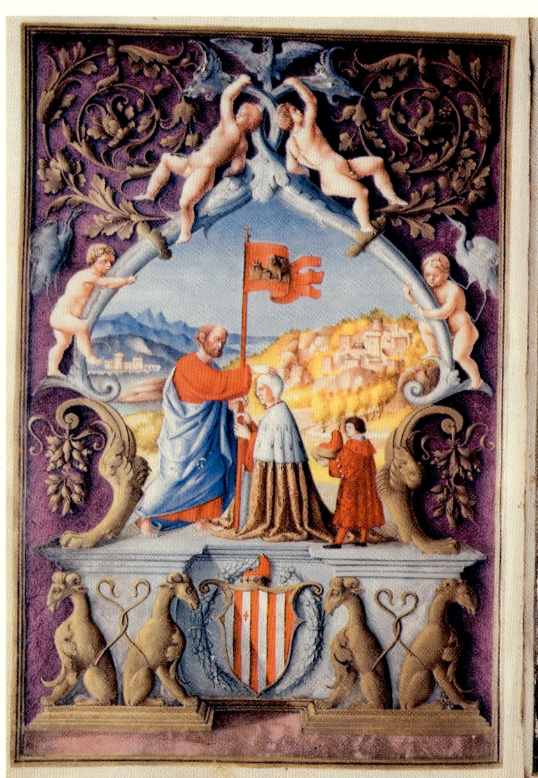

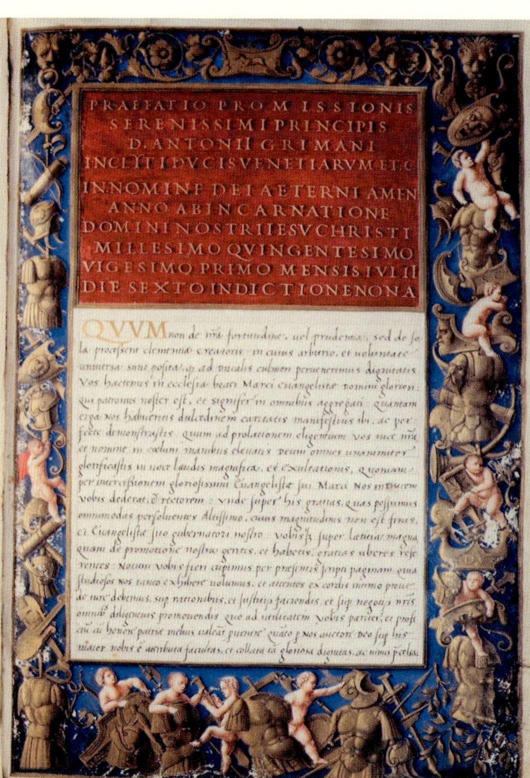

PRAEFATIO PROMISSIONIS
SERENISSIMI PRINCIPIS
D. ANTONII GRIMANI
INCLITI DVCIS VENETIARVM ET C
IN NOMINE DEI AETERNI AMEN
ANNO AB INCARNATIONE
DOMINI NOSTRI IESV CHRISTI
MILLESIMO QVINGENTESIMO
VIGESIMO PRIMO MENSIS IVLII
DIE SEXTO INDICTIONE NONA

QVVM non de nrã fortitudine, uel prudentia, sed de so
la procedent clementia creatoris in cuius arbitrio, et uoluntate
universa sunt posita, q ad ducalis culmen peruenerimus dignitatis
Vos hactenus in ecclesia beati Marci evangelistæ domini gloriosi:
qui patronus noster est, et signifer in omnibus aggregati quantam
erga nos habueritis dulcedinem caritatis manifestius ibi, ac per
fecte demonstrastis quum ad prolationem eligentium vos uice nrã
et nomine in cœlum manibus elevatis deum omnes unanimiter
glorificastis in uoce laudis magnifica, et exultationis, quoniam
per intercessionem gloriosissimi Evangelistæ sui Marci Nos in Ducem
vobis dederat, et rectorem: unde super his gratias, quas possumus
omnimodas persolventes Altissimo, cuius magnitudinis non est finis,
et Evangelistæ suo gubernatori nostro: vobisq super lætitia magna
quam de promotione nostra gentis, et habetis, gratias uberes refe
rentes: Notum vobis fieri cupimus per præsentis scripti paginam, qua
studiosos nos tanto exhibere uolumus, et attentos ex cordis intimo prouí
de tuxe debemus, sup rationibus, et iustitiis faciendis et sup negotiis nris
omnibus diligentius promouendis quo ad utilitatem vobis pariter, et profi
cuũ ac honorẽ patriæ melius valeat puenire quãto p nos auctore deo sup his
maior vobis ẽ attributa facultas, et collata tã gloriosa dignitas, ac nimo pfecta

Afternoon Session

Helena Szépe, Associate Professor of Art at the University of South Florida, was the first speaker of the afternoon session. Helena has been studying Venetian art history since the mid-1980s and has published numerous articles on the subject of Venetian miniature painting and woodcut illustration. Her most recent book, *Venetian Manuscripts and Myths of State,* is about to be published and currently she is collaborating with Lilian Armstrong on another book, entitled *Benedetto Bordon, Master of the Venetian Renaissance Book.*

Helena Szépe's presentation, "Benedetto Bordon and Venetian *Ducali,*" serves a dual purpose in the examination of the early woodcut. First, her talk expands our knowledge of the career of the notable Venetian miniaturist and woodcut designer Benedetto Bordon, also the subject of Lilian Armstrong's presentation in the morning session. Second, she amplifies the work of recent scholars of Venetian history, especially that of Martin Lowry. His book *The World of Aldus Manutius* explores printing history within the larger social and cultural environment of fifteenth- and early sixteenth-century Venice. Taking her cue from Lowry, Szépe focuses her attention on Venetian official manuscript documents called *ducali,* many of which were decorated with illuminations, within the broader context of Venetian political and social history. In doing so she demonstrates the interconnection of this seemingly independent segment of the manuscript market in Venice with early printing. More specifically, her presentation highlights the role that Benedetto Bordon played in both illuminating Venetian *ducali* manuscripts and designing woodcuts for printed books.

Manuscript *ducali* are governmental documents issued by the Venetian Republic that carry the signature of the doge. Szépe focused on three categories of documents,

Promissione of Antonio Grimani, 1521 (London, British Library, Shelfmark Add. 18000 © The British Library, All Rights Reserved).

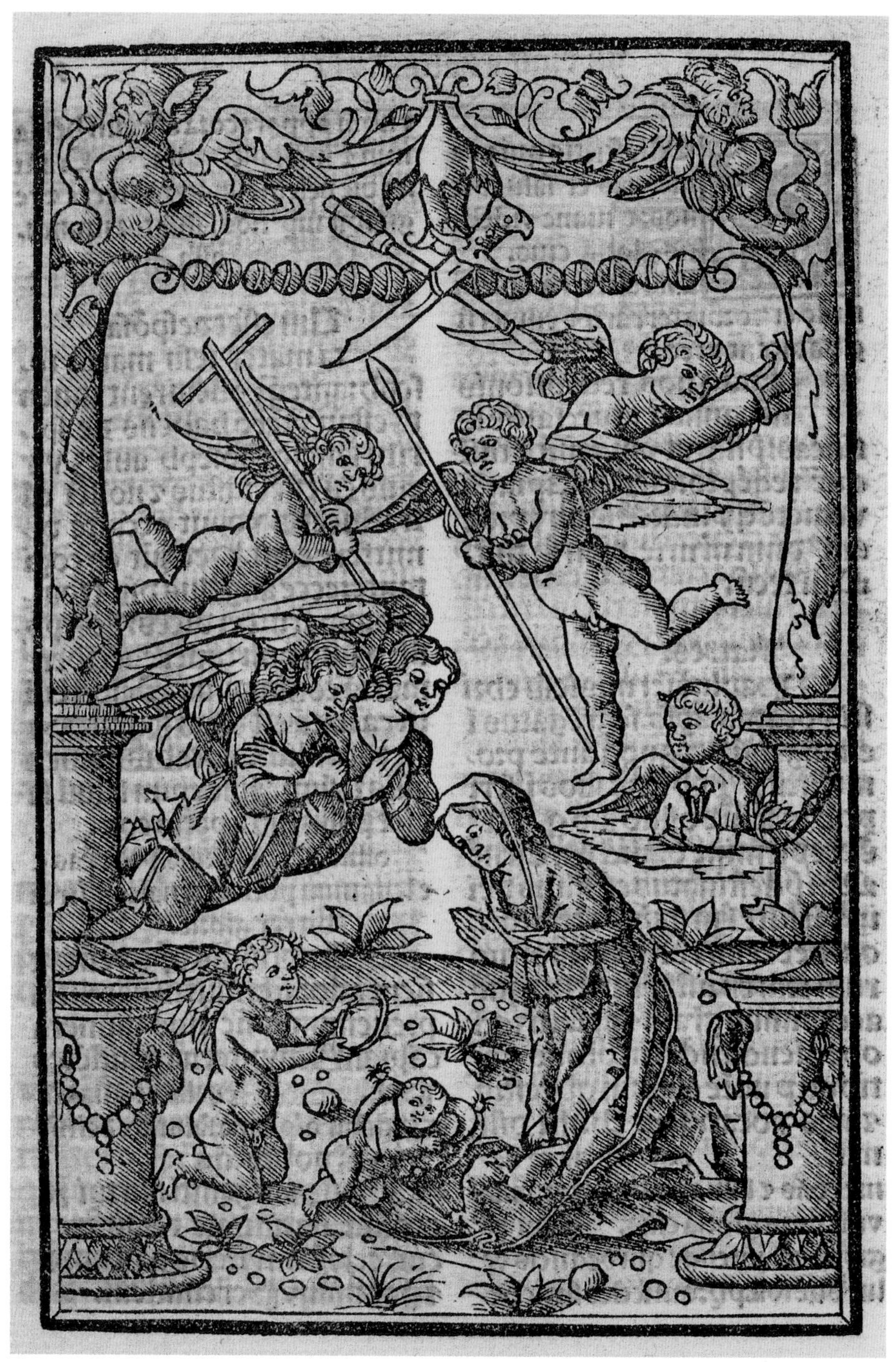

Adoration of Christ, woodcut in *Missale romanum* (Rosenwald Collection 738, Library of Congress, Washington).

ones that were granted to individual patricians outlining the duties and privileges of their appointed offices. *Promissioni* were given to the doge upon his election; the *Giuramento/capitolare* was granted to the procurators, members of the governing council; and the most numerous of these manuscripts, *Commissioni,* were given to governors and captains of Venetian territorial cities. In her examination of these documents, Szépe noticed that over time they were decorated with more and more elaborate miniatures and illuminations, often of excellent quality by known Venetian miniature painters.

As the fifteenth century came to a close, the growing number of illuminated *ducali* reflected the increasing membership in the Great Council of Venice. As their numbers increased, Szépe argues, patricians commissioned elaborately decorated manuscripts to establish their status within the patriciate and to mark for posterity the achievements and position of their family within Venetian society. In the mid-1490s, noted miniature painters like the Master of the Pico Pliny and, a bit later, Benedetto Bordon were commissioned to adorn these documents and enhance the family reputation for posterity. Even with the adoption of the new technology of print, illumination remained a most important means of distinguishing between members of the Venetian ruling class.

Between 1496 and 1528, Benedetto Bordon was the leading miniature painter in Venice. Szépe states that he created *ducali* for the most prestigious positions in the council, testifying to his high reputation among Venetian patricians. She focuses on several *ducali* that demonstrate the progression of Bordon's work over a fifteen-year period. The earliest she mentions was designed around 1496 for Nicolo Leon, who in that year was elected *Procurator de supra.* It follows the general format for depicting St. Mark, set in a landscape holding a book, a design used throughout Italy by many painters of the period. For a *Capitolare* created for Nicolo Michiel of 1500, Bordon illuminated the document with one of his signature motifs, sculpted borders in antique style, imagery he also used in title-page designs for a number of Venetian printers.

The final *ducali* she discusses is a series of illuminations created for Antonio Grimani. Grimani had a tempestuous public career in service to the Republic. He was elected *Procurator de citra* in 1494 but was exiled from Venice in 1500, accused of cowardice in battle when confronted by the Turkish fleet. With the help of his sons, one of whom was Cardinal Domenico Grimani, he was eventually allowed to return to Venice, and in 1510 he regained his former status with an appointment as *Procurator de supra.* Grimani was elected doge in 1521, and the illumination created for his *Promissione* illustrates Bordon's ability to image elements of the investiture ceremony and Venetian patrician ideology. Szépe discusses the controversy over authorship of this illumination, but attributes it to Bordon, and compares the illuminations of this manuscript to the woodcuts of the Giunta Missale (illustrations) to show the close interaction of manuscript and woodcut illustration in Venetian early sixteenth-century books.

Szépe concludes her presentation by suggesting that analysis of these civic documents shows that certain woodcut designers continued to illuminate such manuscripts into the early sixteenth century, revealing a hybrid market for their talents. Because Venetian patricians also patronized artists of monumental painting and sculpture, to glorify themselves and their service to the state, many links between these media and *ducali* miniatures can be found. Benedetto Bordon's imagery influenced the evolution of the Renaissance style and had a lasting impact on illumination and woodcut design well into the sixteenth century.

Eric White, the second speaker, is the Curator of Special Collections at the Bridwell Library, Southern Methodist University, and one of the few rare book curators to hold advanced degrees in both art history and library science. Most recently Eric has written essays about the Gutenberg Bible, the printed editions by Peter Schoeffer, and the rare bookbindings in collections at the Bridwell Library. Before that his contributions were to the field of art history, including studies of Rogier van der Weyden, Hugo van der Goes, Jan van Eyck, and Albrecstht Altdorfer. His presentation, entitled "The Woodcuts in Breydenbach's *Peregrinatio* and the Limits of Fifteenth-Century Empiricism," is an exploration of the imagery created by Erhard Reuwich, the artist who accompanied Breydenbach and made the woodcuts for this seminal travel book about the Holy Lands.

Bernhard von Breydenbach's *Peregrinatio in Terrum Sanctam* is well known to scholars of the Holy Land. It contains a faithful record of his impressions of the cities of the Middle East and the people he encountered during his pilgrimage. It was the first text about the Holy Land printed for a European audience that was based on an eyewitness account and firsthand observations. It also contains a compilation of earlier travel accounts and histories of the Middle East, but these texts were well known at the time and, though important in their own right, did not add to the reservoir of knowledge, as did Breydenbach's account. Reuwich printed the work in Mainz in June of 1486 and illustrated it with twenty-six original woodcuts after his own designs. By 1500 Breydenbach's book had gone through numerous editions and was translated into Latin, German, French, Spanish, and Czech.

As important as Breydenbach's text is, Eric White argues that the "most original and attractive" part of the *Peregrinatio* is its series of woodcut images designed by Reuwich. They were the first woodcuts that rendered the cities of the Middle East and their people in a true-to-life manner. The city scenes were authentic, not imaginary con-

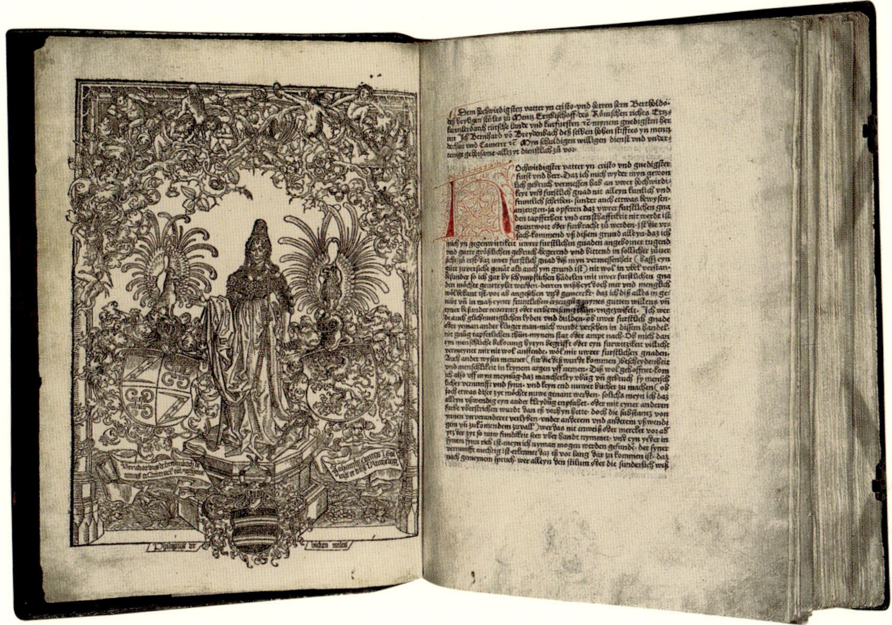

The Woman in the Venetian Dress, woodcut frontispiece in Bernhard von Breydenbach, *Peregrinatio in Terrum Sanctam* (Rosenwald Collection 116, Library of Congress, Washington).

structions like those that were to appear in Schedel's *Nuremberg Chronicle,* printed seven years later. Reuwich's woodcuts also captured the various classes of people in contemporary costume and portrayed a reality not before witnessed by European readers.

White also argues that the work is important because it is the first printed book to be illustrated with foldout images. For example, Reuwich's view of Venice was printed from four blocks on seven folio sheets. The view measures 5 feet 4½ inches long and it folds neatly into the Chancery folio volume that measures about 12 × 8½ inches. His panoramic view of Jerusalem is printed from three blocks on six folios. Candia, Crete, and Rhodes are printed from two blocks on three folios, and so on. Examined today, these views contain many sites still of historical interest and a practiced observer can recognize the architectural skyline of these Middle Eastern cities.

But before examining the views of Venice and Jerusalem more thoroughly, White discusses the remarkable allegorical frontispiece, the Woman in Venetian Dress, that appears at the opening of the book. Various scholars regard the woodcut as the most beautifully rendered image of its type printed by a German during the fifteenth century. It highlights the ability of Reuwich's woodcutter to capture his design by cutting

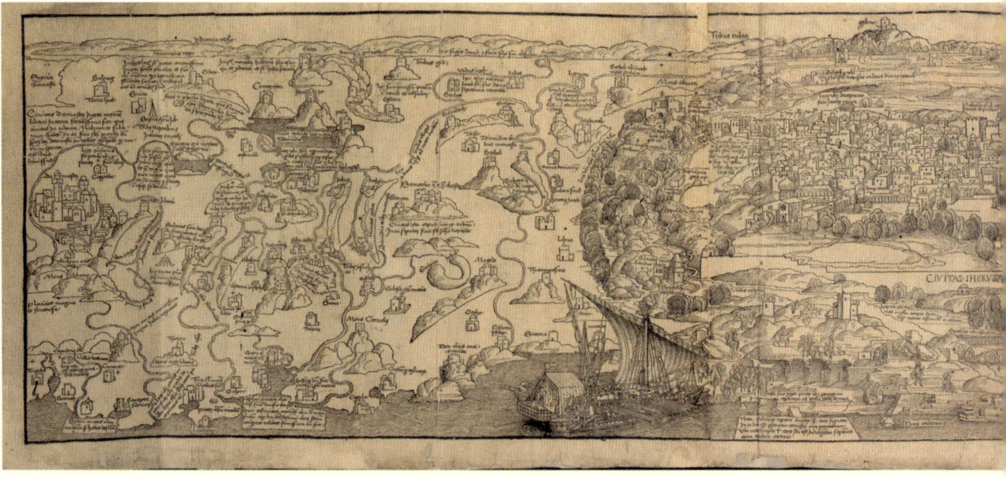

View of Jerusalem, woodcut in Bernhard von Breydenbach, *Peregrinatio in Terrum Sanctam* (Rosenwald Collection 116, Library of Congress, Washington).

intricate patterns and fine line details into the block, techniques that were perfected by Dürer during the next decade. The allegorical image of the Woman in Venetian Dress has been variously described as representing the cities of Mainz, Jerusalem, and Venice, and it has also been suggested that it is a portrait of St. Catherine. White examines each claim and argues with some conviction that "the woman of the *Peregrinatio* personifies the goal of the pilgrimage therein," and represents the city of Jerusalem.

In his discussion of the city view of Venice and the woodcuts representing the courtyard of the Church of the Holy Sepulcher in Jerusalem, a group of Saracen men and women, and exotic animals the travelers came across during their journey, White supports his thesis about the empirical nature of Reuwich's imagery. Citing the amount of information that appears in each image and suggesting comparisons with imagery from other sources, White demonstrates that Reuwich was faithful to his goal of providing accurate depictions of existing monuments for his European audience.

But in Reuwich's panorama of Jerusalem and the Holy Land, White's analysis uncovers a more complex and nuanced rendering that combines accurate depictions of the place with "ingrained political and religious ideologies shared by Breydenbach and his follow pilgrims, and the majority of his European readership." The historic sites of the city and many of its most sacred monuments are defined in Western terms, without acknowledgment of their significance as historic centers of Islamic faith and culture. One of the examples that White focuses on is Temple Mount and its Islamic shrine,

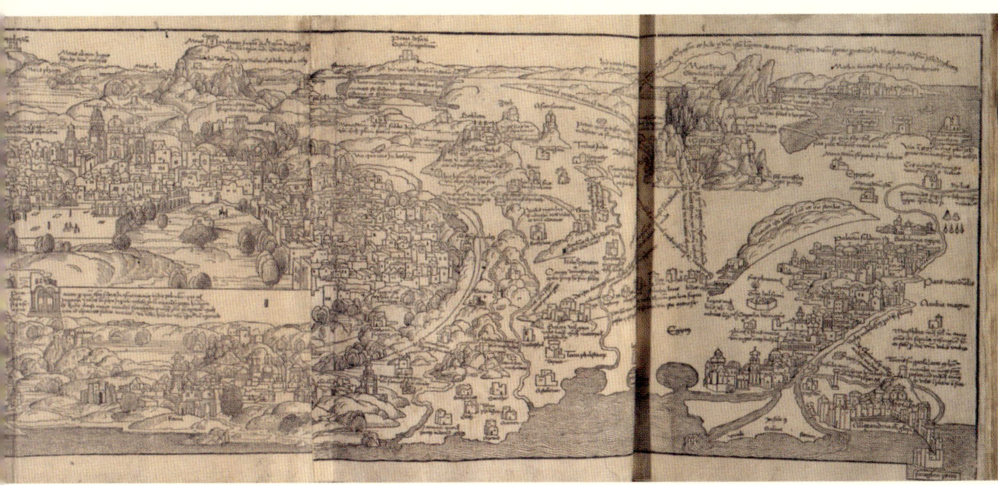

the Dome of the Rock, where Muhammed ascended into heaven. On the panorama, this monument is labeled "Temple of Solomon," referring to the Old Testament temple destroyed in 586 B.C. and familiar to Christians and Jews of all ages. White cites other examples of the Christianization of the Holy Land sites in Reuwich's images and he determines that within the walls of the old City of Jerusalem not one shrine is given its Muslim identity.

White argues that this transposition fulfills the goal of Breydenbach's book, which was to be a guide for Christian pilgrims to the Holy Land. It also demonstrates quite clearly the limits of Reuwich's ability to render the world in purely empirical terms. Though he was one of the first to offer to the world of art historically accurate and factually correct landscapes and cityscapes, he was a man of his place and time in history and representative of its conscious and unconscious worldview.

JEFFREY F. HAMBURGER, the third speaker of the afternoon session, is Professor of Art and Architectural History at the Sackler Museum, Harvard University, and a specialist in Northern European illuminated manuscripts. He is the author of books, articles, essays, and exhibition catalogues on the topic and over the past twenty years has built an impressive body of work. His presentation, "From Print to Manuscript: The Interaction of Incunabula and Illumination after the Invention of Printing," reverses the sequence by which we normally view the relationship between manuscript production and the

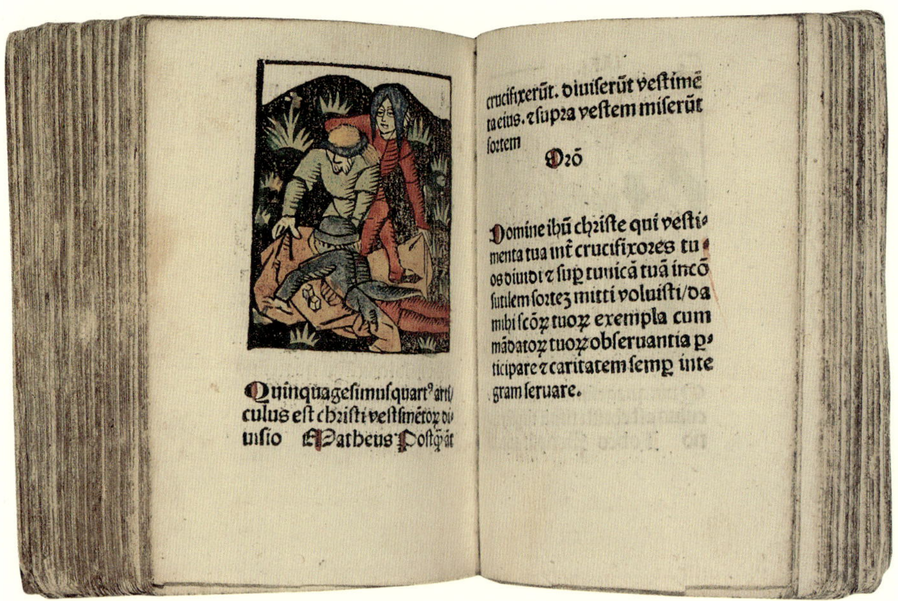

Quinquagesimusquart⁹ arti/
culus est christi vestimētoꝝ di-
uisio Mathëus Postq̄ȝ at

crucifixerūt. diuiserūt vestimē
ta eius. ꝛ supra vestem miserūt
sortem
Orō

Domine ihū christe qui vesti-
menta tua int̄ crucifixores tu-
os diuidi ꝛ sup tunicā tuā incō
sutilem sortez mitti voluisti/da
mihi scōꝝ tuoꝝ exempla cum
mādatoꝝ tuoꝝ obseruantia p-
ticipare ꝛ caritatem semp̄ inte
gram seruare.

Garments of Christ, woodcut in Jordan von Quedlinburg, *Meditationes de vita et passione Jesu Christi* (Rosenwald Collection 545, Library of Congress, Washington).

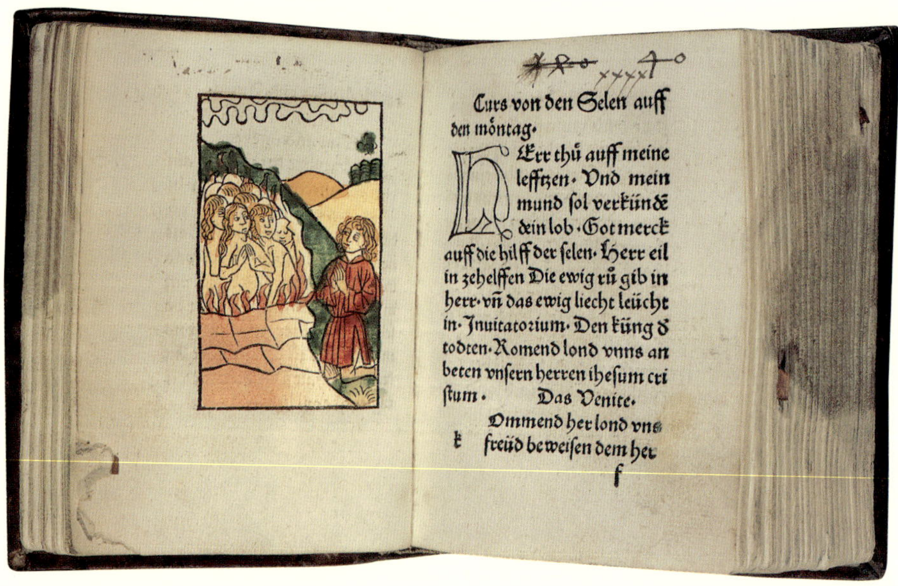

Curs von den Selen auff
den mōntag.
Herr thū auff meine
lefftzen. Vnd mein
mund sol verkünde
dein lob. Got merck
auff die hilff der selen. Herr eil
in zehelffen Die ewig rū gib in
herr. vn̄ das ewig liecht leüchte
in. Inuitatorium. Den küng d
todten. Komend lond vnns an
beten vnsern herren ihesum cri
stum. Das Venite.
Ommend her lond vns
k freüd beweisen dem her
f

Prayers for the Repose of the Souls, woodcut in *Cursus per totam septimanam* (Rosenwald Collection 156, Library of Congress, Washington).

printed book. In this case, Jeffrey Hamburger describes an instance when an illuminated manuscript was modeled after a printed book that contained both an innovative text and a cycle of woodcut illustrations.

The focus of Hamburger's attention is a manuscript fragment of twelve leaves that he was asked to identify. He recognized the illuminations illustrating the fragment as similar to ones that appear in a manuscript volume in the Houghton Library at Harvard University. The volume is a part of the Divine Office called a *Matutinale,* a section of the service book containing only the prayers for Matins. The *Matutinale* may come from the Dominican convent in Unterlinden in Colmar, and after a close comparison Hamburger attributed the fragment also to Unterlinden. In addition, he suggested that, given the similarities between the two manuscripts, both were written and decorated by the same scribe.

His examination of the fragment also suggested that its text was based on prayers from Jordan of Quedlinburg's *Meditationes,* or *Articles of the Passion,* written in the fourteenth century. The text is known in over one hundred manuscript copies and nine editions were printed before 1501. What puzzled Hamburger about the fragment was that each of the twelve prayers is accompanied by an illumination. The complete work of the *Articles of the Passion* includes sixty-five prayers. Given clues visible in the physical structure of the fragment, if complete it would have at least fifty-nine prayers with corresponding illuminations. In all his experience, Hamburger had come across only one manuscript of the *Articles* that included a complete cycle of illuminations, but that was dated 1518. He was familiar with a 1458 devotional miscellany that showed evidence that at one time it carried a cycle of prints for each of the liturgical divisions of the *Articles,* but all the prints, probably woodcuts, had since been removed. Thus he states, "Against this foil provided by sporadically illustrated manuscripts such as these, not to mention the vast number lacking illustrations of any kind, the fragments in Colmar stand out as anomalous on account of their extensive, if not complete, cycle of images."

In order to account for the anomaly, Hamburger compared the fragment with a printed edition of the *Articles.* The first printed edition of Jordan of Quedlinburg's *Articles of the Passion* appeared in 1485. The printer Gerard Leeu of Antwerp issued subsequent editions in 1487, 1488, and 1491. Leeu's edition of the *Articles* was illustrated with seventy-five woodcuts using fifty-eight different woodblocks. All of the sixty-five prayers were illustrated, as were the chapter openings that separated different parts of the text. The work was very successful, no doubt because of its illustrations, and printers in Lübeck and Magdeburg copied Leeu's format and produced editions in 1491 and 1500, respectively. A copy of the 1488 edition printed by Gerard Leeu appears in the exhibition *A Heavenly Craft.* It is bound with a unique copy of a fully illustrated edition of the *Rosarium Beate Virginae Maria* printed by Leeu in 1489.

Early books printed north of the Alps, especially prayer books and devotional texts, oftentimes were illustrated with woodcut images. Hamburger cites another example from *A Heavenly Craft,* the *Dye Siben Cursz* printed in Ulm by Conrad Dinckmut in 1491. Dinckmut illustrated his edition with seven images, one for each division of the text, a normal convention used by fifteenth-century printers for devotional books of this type: seven woodcuts printed as contemplative guides for each day of the week, or perhaps fourteen cuts that focused prayer and meditation on the Stations of the Cross. In the 1480s it was very unlikely that a printer would use anywhere near the number of images that Leeu used for his simple prayer book, and this innovation was reflected in the format that appeared in the fragment prayer book.

Hamburger compared the written text in the Colmar fragment with the printed text that appears in Leeu's edition of the *Articles.* He determined that the scribe copied his manuscript from one of the editions of Leeu's prayer book. He made this judgment based on the changes to the text of Jordan of Quedlinburg that appears in both the printed book and the fragment. The prayers deviate substantially from all known manuscript texts of the *Articles.* Leeu abridged each to the length of a short prayer or heading, providing just enough information to identify the image, which became the focus of the reader. Gone were lengthy commentaries and quotations from the early Church Fathers that Quedlinburg used to elucidate points for specific meditation. In their place were woodcut images forming the context for prayer, without justification or doctrinal support. Leeu's achievement, copied by the scribe who produced the Colmar fragment, was to place an image on the verso of one leaf opposite an abridged text printed on the verso of the next. Thus for each opening, the image was merely informed by a few lines of text, "thereby enhancing the importance of the pictures" for Leeu's printed edition and the subsequent manuscript produced at the Dominican convent of Unterlinden.

Hamburger goes on to state that the use of one image for every article was unprecedented for its time. But as closely as the scribe followed Leeu's text and format, he completely ignored the iconographical content of the woodcut images that appear in the printed edition. It is of course impossible to know exactly how many images were created for the complete manuscript, but given what we know, there must have been at least fifty illustrations in the complete work. The sources for these images, based on the twelve that Hamburger examined, have not been identified and the limits of our knowledge about the fragment have, at this juncture, been reached. It could be that the scribe used various engravings, single-leaf woodcuts, or other manuscript

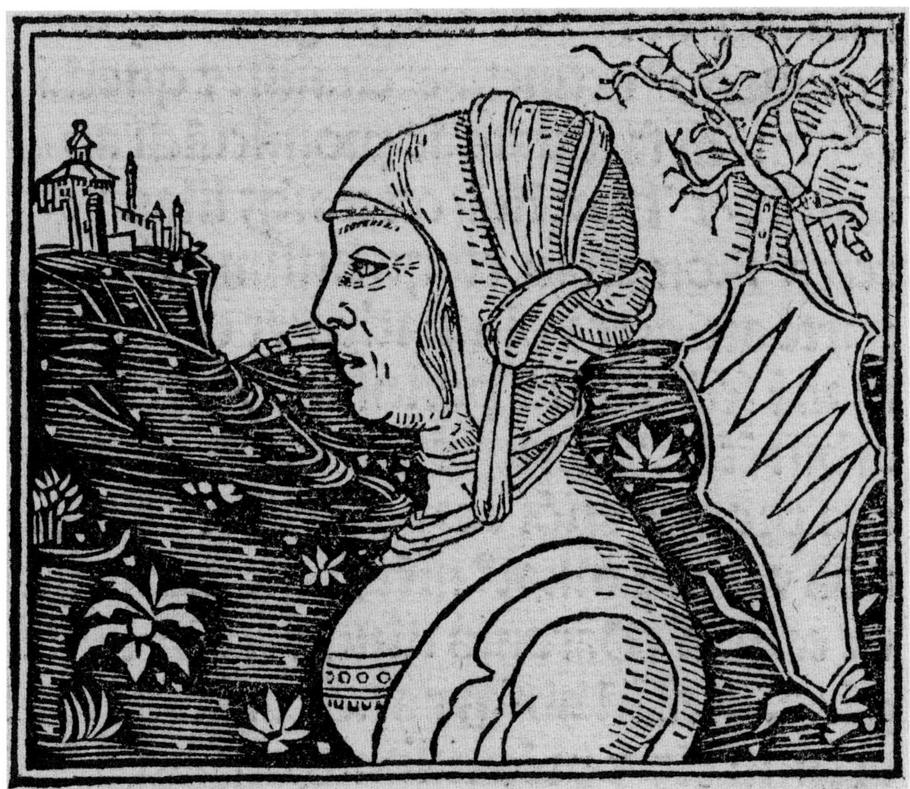

Genevra Bentivoglio, woodcut in Jacopo Filippo Foresti, *De claris mulieribus* (Rosenwald Collection 323, Library of Congress, Washington).

images as his models, but no series as extensive as the one created for Leeu are known. What is known is that the Colmar fragment is not rooted in a tradition of manuscripts. Rather it was based on a printed book that served as the model of an innovative way of combining image and text, "in short, new ways of seeing."

DANIEL DE SIMONE, the final speaker of the day, is curator of the Lessing J. Rosenwald Collection at the Library of Congress. The topic of his paper, "The Woodcut in Ferrara in the Late Fifteenth Century," was formulated while writing descriptions for the exhibition catalogue *A Heavenly Craft: The Woodcut in Early Printed Books.* He cautioned his audience that his work was speculative at the moment but that he hoped to develop it into a detailed study of the evolution of the Ferrarese woodcut style at the end of the fifteenth century.

De Simone begins with a brief chronology of printing in Ferrara. The first printer was Andreas Belfortis, whose career lasted from 1471 until 1493. The first illustrated book did not appear until 1479, when Augustino Canerio printed an edition of

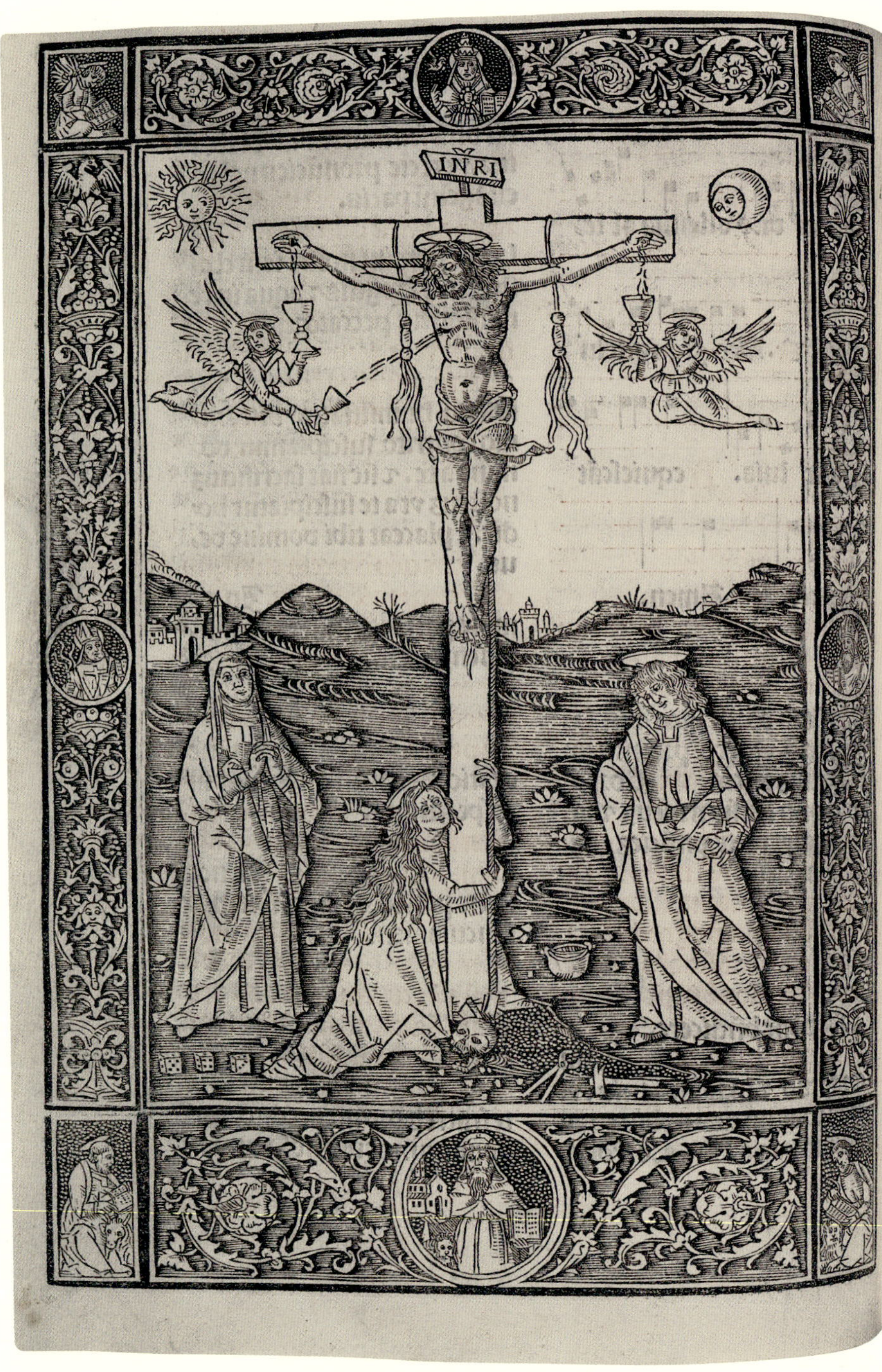

Crucifixion, canon cut *Missale secundū ordinem Carthusiensium* (Rosenwald Collection 744, Library of Congress, Washington).

the *Constitutiones* of Pope Clement V. It contains one small rectangular image of the pope seated between two cardinals. The figures are set in natural poses and look quite comfortable, and Pope Clement is rendered with an expressive countenance. It was cut in simple outline and displays a lightness of hand that gives the design an open feel. It was to be ten years before the next illustrated book appeared in Ferrara and it came from the press of Lorenzo di Rossi, the most heralded Ferrarese printer of the period.

For the remainder of his presentation De Simone concentrates on four of Lorenzo di Rossi's most important illustrated books. He examines the woodcut portrait that appeared in di Rossi's *Legenda di San Maurellio* of 1489. The image shows the influences of Cosmé Tura, the noted mid-fifteenth-century painter from Ferrara. By examining the architectural elements, the composition of the design, and the rendering of the garments of San Maurellio, and comparing them to elements that appear in paintings by Tura, De Simone demonstrates a probable source for the woodcut portrait.

He follows with a series of images that appear in *De claris mulierbus* by Johannes Phillipus di Bergomensis and the *Epistles* of Saint Jerome, both printed by Lorenzo di Rossi in 1497. De Simone attempts to demonstrate how the woodcuts in these two works are essential to understanding the emergence of a Ferrarese style that appeared so dramatically in the edition of the *Missale secundum* printed in 1503.

He focuses first on the *Epistles* of St. Jerome, which was illustrated with two full-page monumental woodcuts, enclosed with architectural borders, and a series of 180 small column cuts inserted into the text. He points out that the format of this folio volume, with its double columns of type, is typical of the harmonious style of Venetian printing. He also notes how similar the cuts were to those that appear in editions of the Malermi Bible and the *Divine Comedy,* both printed in Venice in 1491. The design of these cuts have been attributed to the Pico Master, and De Simone cites research by Lilian Armstrong on the Venetian miniature painter, who made the transition from the manuscript trade to the print trade in the early 1490s. Armstrong has suggested, based on stylistic elements in his work, that the Pico Master may have trained as a miniature painter in Ferrara as a young man, and returned there in 1495 after finishing his career in Venice as an illuminator and woodcut designer. The designs that appear in these full-page cuts and the column cuts do reflect elements of style attributed to the Pico Master and he could be the source of woodcuts that appear in the 1497 *Epistle* of St. Jerome.

The 173 woodcut portraits that appear in *De claris mulierbus* reflect a more varied series of stylistic elements coming from Venetian, Florentine, and Ferrarese sources. De Simone again mentions the full-page woodcuts that appear in both these works, suggesting a Venetian connection, but he focuses most of his attention on the portrait blocks and their varied styles. He offers examples that illustrate Florentine characteristics, including the natural presentation of the figures, their developed facial features, their distinctive costumes, and their evocative expressions. Specifically, he discusses the compositional formats of the eight portraits of contemporary Italian women and offers examples of the paintings by Ercole di Roberti, the Ferrarese painter, that were the probable sources for these likenesses. He also refers to other influences appearing in these woodcut portraits, including ones that could be most clearly seen in the full-page woodcut of the Crucifixion that appeared in the Carthusian missal that was printed in Ferrara in 1503.

Although Lorenzo de Rossi's name does not appear in the book, De Simone cites previous bibliographical research that links di Rossi to the printing of the 1503 *Missale secundum*. It contains an evocative full-page image of the Crucifixion, distinctive for the technique used by the cutter to embellish the design. It contains a highly sculpted background of striated black-on-white lines that seem to shimmer around the vertical thrust of the cross. This technique also appears in many of the portraits in the *De claris mulierbus.* The background effect gives the central focus of the image a prominence that appears in few other woodcuts from the period. In addition to the striated lines, the design contains a particularly sensitive rendering of the image of Mary, Saint John, and Mary Magdalene positioned at the foot of the cross. In particular, the rendering of Mary Magdalene with her woeful expression and arms wrapped around the base of the cross carries a powerful emotional punch, and the woodcut as whole draws the viewer into the scene.

For De Simone these choices reflect an individual creativity that emanates from the skills of the cutter, who formed a startling translation from a well-established design. He concludes that a great part of the Ferrarese style that emerges in this 1503 missal may be based on the particular skills of the woodcutter, a craftsman who was able to synthesize a variety of stylistic elements from Venetian, Florentine, and Ferrarese paintings and miniatures and turn them into an original style that emerged in Ferrara at the beginning of the sixteenth century.

Contributors

RICHARD S. FIELD is Curator Emeritus of Prints, Drawings, and Photographs at Yale University Gallery. From 1962 to 1968 he served as Acting Curator of the Lessing J. Rosenwald Collection at Alverthrope in Jenkintown, Pennsylvania. In 1965 for the National Gallery of Art he published his first major work, *Fifteenth Century Woodcuts and Metalcuts,* presenting the first systematic analysis of the woodcut prints in the Rosenwald Collection. Over the course of a nearly forty-five-year career, he has produced books, articles, and exhibition pieces on a wide variety of subjects, including Jasper Johns, Paul Gauguin, the prints of Gabriel de Saint-Aubin, Walker Evans, and Rembrandt, and written important surveys of American prints and watercolors, allegorical prints, and the development of the photographic tradition in the American West.

LILIAN ARMSTRONG is the Mildred Lane Kemper Professor of Art at Wellesley College. Her areas of scholarly specialization are Venetian art, northern Italian manuscripts, and early printed books. She has published two books on north Italian painting and book illumination, *The Painting and Drawings of Marco Zoppo* (1976) and *Renaissance Miniature Painters and Classical Imagery: the Master of the Putti and His Venetian Workshop* (1981). She is also a coauthor of *The Painted Page: Italian Renaissance Book Illumination 1450–1995,* the catalogue of an exhibition at the Royal Academy of Arts London and at the Pierpont Morgan Library, New York, in 1994–1995. She has contributed numerous articles to scholarly journals on Renaissance book decoration.

PETER STALLYBRASS is the Walter H. and Leonore C. Annenberg Professor in the Humanities and Professor of English at the University of Pennsylvania and codirector of the Penn Humanities Forum. He is a noted scholar of the Renaissance, the history of the book, and material culture. He received the James Russell Lowell Prize of the Modern Language Association for his book *Renaissance Clothing and the Materials of*

Memory with Ann Rosalind Jones. His other books include *The Politics and Poetics of Transgression* with Allon White and *O Casaco de Marx: Roupas, Memria, Dor,* a collection of essays on Marx, materiality, and memory.

HELENA SZÉPE is Associate Professor of Art at the University of South Florida at Tampa. Her research examines the place of books in the visual culture of Venice from the fourteenth to the sixteenth centuries. She is the author of numerous articles and reviews on Venetian printing and illuminated manuscripts which have appeared in journals such as *I Tatti Studies, Word and Image, Papers of the Bibliographical Society of Canada, Renaissance Quarterly,* and *The Book Collector.*

ERIC MARSHALL WHITE is Curator of Special Collections at Bridwell Library, Southern Methodist University. His research has focused mainly on fifteenth-century printing. His publications include an in-depth commentary for the CD-ROM facsimile of the Gutenberg Bible at the University of Texas, Austin (2005), two articles in *Gutenberg-Jahrbuch* (2002 and 2006), and the catalogues for the Bridwell exhibitions "Peter Schoeffer: Printer of Mainz" (2003) and "Six Centuries of Master Bookbinding at Bridwell Library" (2006). He is currently compiling a digital image-census of all the vellum fragments of the Gutenberg Bible and an annotated census of all documented fifteenth-century edition sizes.

JEFFREY F. HAMBURGER, Professor of Art History at Harvard University, is the author of *Nuns as Artists, The Visual and the Visionary: Art and Female Spirituality in Late Medieval Germany, The Rothschild Canticles,* and *St. John the Divine: The Deified Evangelist in Medieval Art and Theology.* He coedited (with Anne-Marie Bouché) *The Mind's Eye: Art and Theological Argument in the Medieval West.* Among his areas of special interest are medieval manuscript illumination, text-image issues, the history of attitudes towards imagery and, more broadly, visual experience, and German vernacular religious writing of the Middle Ages, especially in the context of mysticism.

DANIEL DE SIMONE has been Curator of the Lessing J. Rosenwald Collection at the Library of Congress since January 2000. During the previous twenty-five years spent in the rare book trade, he owned his own business and helped build collections for both private collectors and rare book libraries. He has written many sales catalogues and articles on book-related subjects. He edited the exhibition catalogue *A Heavenly Craft: The Woodcut in Early Printed Books,* which describes some of the illustrated books donated by Lessing Rosenwald to the Library of Congress.

Index

Page numbers in *italics* refer to illustrations.